C000154179

THE DI

CAULDRON

Memories Of A Desert Rat

PETE MERRILL

APS PUBLICATIONS

The Devil's Cauldron
Copyright ©2017 APS Publications

Cover illustrations by Rik Rawling

APS Publications,
4 Oakleigh Road,
Stourbridge,
West Midlands,
DY8 2JX

www.andrewsparke.com

"I found myself in the middle of this duel, very exposed and scared. My position received two direct hits."
- Fred Pattinson

Despite my years of experience as a military historian, nothing could have prepared me for the ride I would go on when I met Fred Pattinson – a WW2 veteran, who had bravely volunteered for military service at the start of the war, despite being too young.

His request that I help him find his lost war medals quickly turned into a journey through his life in the army, during one of the most infamous conflicts the world has ever seen.

Journey with Fred as he moves from anti-aircraft duty in Birmingham, to the deserts of North Africa and Palestine, volunteering for various duties along the way. His extraordinary stories remind us of the unimaginable experiences which war veterans endured, and which military personnel still endure, to guarantee our freedom.

This book is the culmination of months of work with Fred to help him share his experiences with today's generation, and future generations to come.

Curious about whether Fred was reunited with his medals? I hope that you will read on to find out for yourself.

To Margaret
When everything under the sun appears to be going wrong and my whole world is crashing down, I stop and ask myself a simple question: do I have water and you by my side?
If the answer is yes, then everything will be okay!

CONTENTS

Preface

My hobby is trading and selling military medals. This involves buying medals, then researching the recipient's military service to add provenience and, with some luck, added value, before selling them on. This research process has turned me into an amateur military historian, which has in turn resulted in requests to help people explore the military careers of their family members and relatives, or to help recover lost medals.

My past research results have often been summarised in a few pages in the format of a short storyboard. When a more detailed description is provided, it is sometimes possible to produce a booklet. Occasionally, as in this case, I come across an enthralling story with the breadth and depth to be developed into something even more substantial.

This story started in June 2013, when I received a familiar request. I was asked "Can you help locate the missing medals belonging to my Uncle Fred?" Unusually for me, the recipient was still alive and we arranged to meet to see if I could help. All I had been told was that he had served in World War II but at our first meeting, before we even spoke, I made two assumptions. Firstly, I thought that he had been a 'Desert Rat' and served for a long period in North Africa, and that he had been in the Royal Artillery. My first assumption was based on the scarring on his head and face, caused by treatment for skin cancer; this type of scarring is a familiar sight on veterans of all nationalities who served in the region. I also presumed that he had served in the Royal Artillery because he wore hearing aids; many veterans suffer hearing loss late in life. I was correct about North Africa and right, by chance, about the artillery; he had served with the artillery, but his deafness was not related to guns, and instead had resulted from foundry work after the war. It turned out that he had misplaced his medals many years ago and had hoped to wear them again on Remembrance Day that coming November.

I committed to finding replacement medals for Fred if he, in return, would tell me all about his experiences and let me write them down. I have written extensively about North Africa but not had the opportunity to speak at length with someone who served throughout the campaign. Fred agreed, and that is how it all began.

Many people performed extraordinary feats of bravery and lived through an astonishing array of campaigns during the long years of the Second World War, yet few saw as much action or witnessed as much misery as Fred Pattinson.

I was fortunate and privileged to be able to go on this journey with Fred, which consisted of many hours sat by the fire at his home drinking countless cups of 'Char'. I also felt honoured to accompany him on trips to and from hospital to visit his wife Margaret and, towards the end, was lucky to visit him at his care home. We would discuss each chapter in turn; I would go away and undertake the background research, then we would revisit the narrative and any memories that had surfaced would be included. Once he was happy with the account, we moved onto the next. We laughed, cried and sometimes just sat in silence together whilst he remembered events he had long buried. There was more than one occasion when I wondered if this project was wise, as the memories often appeared too painful. Fred was insistent that he would tell me his story, but it should be recorded in a way that would be readable for teenagers, who he felt had little understanding of what he and others had endured to ensure that they have the freedom they have today.

It was a long and rewarding process, but not without challenges. The golden thread that runs through the story is Fred's war memories. However, time can play tricks on even the sharpest of memories, and this meant that the war stories Fred recalled were often mixed-up. The order of events, activity, dates and places had become a jumble in his memory, and he was often steadfast in his belief that his accounts were accurate. The critical ingredients that helped to unravel and authenticate the story were Fred's service records, his war diaries from the various units he served in around the world, and other contemporary records. These were all invaluable aids which allowed him to recall events accurately. What this book contains is Fred's story, in his own words, as he told it to me.

I could not end this preface without acknowledging the immeasurable assistance given to me by Ann Swabey during the process of compiling this account; her help in gathering the research material was vital. In addition, I must thank the Royal Artillery Museum, National Archive, Imperial War Museum, and the Commonwealth War Graves Commission for making available documentation to aid with piecing together the official version of events.

"While Fred is no longer with us, I feel privileged to have spent so much time with him, and will always be grateful, as we all are, that he and his comrades were in the right place, at the right time."
Pete Merrill 2017

1
War Clouds Gather

My mother died when I was twelve, so I had to move in with my grandparents. They lived in a small tied cottage just on the outskirts of the village of Greatgate in Staffordshire, some forty miles north of Birmingham.

The First World War was still fresh in everyone's minds; being born soon after it had ended meant that I'd grown up hearing of its horrors and the lost family members, and seeing ex-servicemen with missing limbs begging in the street.

In 1935, I left school at age fourteen, which was normal then, and started working on a local farm, six days a week as a labourer. I would start well before the crack of dawn, and work until around four in the afternoon, with the exception of harvest time, when everyone worked until the light had gone. Farming was very primitive by today's standards; there was very little petrol machinery around, with just shire-horses used to pull and drag. I became very accomplished with these one-ton beasts which, despite their size, had a gentle temperament. I did everything from ploughing, harrowing, muck spreading, fertilising, sowing, planting, hoeing, weeding, digging ditches, harvesting, carting, threshing, stacking, thatching, tending livestock, and even rat and mole-catching.

It was hard work for not much pay. I was earning around one pound and ten shillings a week, or less if the weather was too bad to work all day, as the farmer never paid for lost hours.

My only time off from work came on Christmas Day and Boxing Day. Lunch was called *dockey*, and typically consisted of half a loaf of bread with a chunk of cheese or pork washed down with a bottle of ale.

In 1938, Germany invaded Austria and was making plans to invade Czechoslovakia; everyone was talking of war. In September, the Prime Minister, Neville Chamberlain, flew to see Hitler and his gang and signed an agreement in an attempt to prevent war. Chamberlain came back in triumph holding a piece of paper, and announced: "I have returned from Germany with peace for our time." It was all rubbish; nobody trusted Hitler or his agreement, but it did give us time to churn out planes, ships, and tanks, and prepare for war.

In spring 1939, the war clouds were gathering; I was now seventeen and no longer living with my grandparents. My father had retired from the police force and he and my brother, Ernest, had now moved in with them. I was still a farm labourer, but was working and living on a farm in Tean, some three miles away. On a Sunday, after I had completed the morning milking, I would walk the three miles home to get my laundry done and have Sunday lunch with the family before returning to the farm in the evening.

The atmosphere was out of the ordinary to say the least. By now, we had all been issued gas masks, identity cards, and ration books, and at the farm and at my grandparents' house, we had built Anderson air raid shelters, which were buried in the back gardens.

The government had introduced the Military Training Act, and all men between the ages of twenty and twenty-one had to register for six months' military training. Later, in October, this changed to conscription, which meant compulsory enlistment into the armed services for men between twenty and twenty-three.

As a farm labourer, I was working in what was known as a *reserved occupation*, which was seen as essential to the war effort, and so I was exempt, or rather forbidden, from being conscripted.

It was on Sunday, 3rd September 1939, just after my eighteenth birthday, that the inevitable happened and Germany invaded Poland. Chamberlain announced over the radio that we were now at war with Germany and we all cheered.

Reality hit home when, at 9.20 a.m. on the 16th October 1939, German bombers appeared over the Forth Bridge in Scotland and bombed warships lying in Queensferry Docks. After that, preparations for air attacks were intensified throughout the country and the war suddenly seemed very much closer.

Before the war, Britain imported fifty-five million tons of food each year; by the end of 1939, this had dropped to twelve million due to the German blockade around our shores. There was talk of a possible famine and Churchill said that if necessary, "Food supplies could take priority over supplies for the military."

I guess this did make me feel that I was doing an important job by working on the farm, but, what I really wanted to do was to *get some in*.

On the 10th May 1940, just after the fall of France, Chamberlain resigned his premiership and was succeeded by Winston Churchill. Sadly, Chamberlain died of cancer six months later. By June, the war in France was not going very well, with British and French soldiers having to be evacuated from Dunkirk. It was at this time that Churchill gave his famous speech: "This was their finest hour...the Battle of France is over. I expect that the Battle of Britain is about to begin."

Hitler believed that, with our defeat on the continent and without any European allies, an armistice with Britain would soon follow. Fortunately, he got that wrong!

It was the English Channel that halted the Germans; they only made preparations for a land campaign, and were not equipped for an amphibious assault on Britain.

In July, Hitler ordered the preparation of a plan to invade Britain: *Directive number 16*. He also hoped that news of the preparations would frighten Churchill into peace negotiations. He was wrong on this account also!

What it did do was make the country prepare for invasion; road signs were taken down and we all watched the sky, expecting enemy paratroopers to descend at any time.

Hitler's grand invasion plan was code-named *Operation Sea Lion*, and was scheduled to take place in mid-September. He knew it would not be possible to carry out a successful amphibious assault on Britain until the RAF had been neutralised. Hitler also believed that, if the attacks on military targets failed, then bombing civilians could force the British government to surrender. He was wrong yet again!

Birmingham was not too far away, and due to its industrial importance and contribution to the war effort, it came as no surprise when it was targeted by the German Luftwaffe. Vickers-Armstrong at Castle Bromwich was mass-producing the Spitfire fighter aircraft, while the Longbridge car plant had already switched to the production of munitions and military equipment. The Longbridge factory produced ammunition, mines and depth charges, as well as tank suspensions, and even steel helmets. Later, they would also produce Hurricane fighters and Airspeed Horsa gliders.

The first bombs hit Birmingham on the 9th August 1940, and targeted the Gravelly Hill and Short Heath areas of Erdington. This was followed by nothing for four days, but from the 13th onwards, the Blitz started. It was relentless, night after night.

It is a strange experience, lying in the dark and listening to the sound of planes overhead, not knowing if their bombs will land on you or not. We would watch the searchlights fingering the clouds and, now and then, sometimes close at hand, sometimes far away, a bomb would drop and the windows would rattle. The anti-aircraft guns would become active, making a 'pop-pop-pop' noise. The next

day on the 9 a.m. radio we were told that so many...enemy planes were shot down during the night'.

2
The King's Shilling

I had already been contemplating joining-up for some considerable time. I even thought about the Home Guard, or 'Dad's Army', as it became known. But my age and the fact that I was working in a reserved occupation were both against me. The nightly air raids on Birmingham made me more determined than ever, but I knew that if my ambition was to be fulfilled it would mean lying about my age and occupation. Lying to the authorities was something I did not necessarily want to do.

However, in August, just days after the first bombs fell on Birmingham, myself and my pal, Reg Pedge, presented ourselves at the recruitment centre in Longton, Stoke-on-Trent to enlist; my choice was the navy.

The Sergeant asked me my age. "Twenty sir," I said, and he laughed and asked to see my birth certificate. "Lost sir," I said.

So, rather than lying, I told him my true age and occupation. Now, the next bit is a little complicated, but a lesson in how creative the military mind can be! Although the conscription rule was that I needed to be twenty, it could potentially be interpreted as *twenty before you can see combat*.

The sums were simple; the next draft was going to be in December, followed by two months' basic training and two months' specialist trade training, making April the *combat* month. I therefore needed to be twenty in April of 1941.

However, I was three months short, and so the sergeant changed my birthday by four months, with a few days added on for good measure. He then declared my occupation as a 'general labourer' rather than a farm labourer. Easy as that!

Although when I walked in I had wanted to join the navy, somewhere amongst the lies and deception I ended up in the army! I signed up there and then, took the *King's Shilling*, and went home to wait for my call-up papers.

I later learned that when no proof of age is provided, the military gets around the issue with equally simple ingenuity — through a medical examination. All the medical officer had to do was sign the recruitment documentation confirming 'apparent' age, based on physical development following an examination.

As for my pal Reg, he never got through the military medical because of his poor eyesight. He ended up going to America to help prepare planes.

When I told my father what I had done, he was indifferent but supportive; I was just grateful that any lies to get me in had come from the recruiter and not myself, as he would have disapproved.

I did not have to wait too long before the papers arrived, telling me to report to Hanley on the 30th October for a medical. I arrived in good time and was examined by a Major Haglewood, of the Royal Army Medical Corps. The whole thing was rudimentary; shirt off, listen to my chest, eye test, watch the cold hands and cough. "You'll do, NEXT!"

We then moved to the next room and together with the other new recruits, I took an oath of allegiance; "Hold up your right hand, and repeat after me..."

I was now Gunner 1595592, Fredrick Arthur Pattinson, Royal Artillery. I was given a railway pass and told to report to Devizes railway station at eleven a.m. on the 12th December, where I would be joining the 207th Anti-Aircraft Training Regiment, Royal Artillery, at Roundway Camp; I was also told "Don't be late."

Until then it was back to working on the farm. On one occasion, I was helping to deliver milk and eggs to a local shopkeeper in Tean who was well- known for being a late payer. When we arrived, there was no sign of the shopkeeper, just his son minding the store. I asked if we could have the milk and egg money that was due from the last delivery. He replied, 'Father's out and Mother's ill in bed and I don't have any money'.

At that very moment, a number of people came into the shop asking if they could buy a bed or mattress or something to sleep on, as their home had been damaged in an air raid. The lad replied that they had none because there had been a run on these items due to the Blitz, but that his father was trying to obtain more supplies. It was at this point that the shopkeeper suddenly appeared and promptly got his wife out of her sick bed before selling it, still warm, so as not to miss out on a sale. I do not know what happened to his wife but at least he was able to pay his bill and we returned to the farm, cash in hand.

On another occasion, after delivering milk and eggs, we were returning to the farm. It was almost dark and we were stopped by the local constable outside his police house. He informed us that we were not using the headlight cover correctly on the van and any German planes could spot it from the air and ascertain our location. This, he told us, was an offence and he would have to *book us*!

At this point, the policeman's wife came out to see who her husband was talking to. Realising it was us, she asked if she could have some milk and eggs, as she wanted to do a batch of baking. She rushed into the house and returned with two large jugs for the milk and a bowl for the eggs. Quick as a flash, we filled the jugs and bowl and then asked for his police helmet for some additional eggs. Then, with his and his wife's hands full, he was unable to do anything about the original incident for fear of spilling the milk or breaking the eggs, and so we drove off quickly, leaving the policeman red-faced. Some weeks later, he caught up with us and reminded us of the offence. But we reminded him that he had not paid for the milk or eggs, and that was the last we heard of the incident.

3
Basic Training

On the 11th December 1940, Birmingham was subjected to a relentless thirteen-hour raid by 200 German bombers. How they kept the trains, or anything, going after that I do not know, but they did! I arrived at Devizes station late in the afternoon, which was later than my orders had stated. I found a crowd of lost souls like myself, milling about trying to keep warm and out of the drizzle whilst waiting for somebody to bring order to the chaos. This someone eventually arrived in the shape of a smartly-turned-out corporal who promptly bellowed out, "GET FELL IN".

This, of course was meaningless to us, but he soon had us herded outside and formed-up into some sort of order. He then marched us in the fading light and drizzle, two miles down London Road to Le Marchant Barracks. These barracks, as well as Roundway Camp, became my new home for the next four months.

It was now getting late, and after being broken up into groups of thirty, we were shown into our barrack rooms. There we found that our beds merely consisted of three boards resting on two small trestles about nine inches above the ground. They looked decidedly uncomfortable. However, we were then marched across to a huge barn containing a pile of canvas palliasse sacks and bales of straw. We each had to pick up a palliasse, fill it with straw to make our mattresses, and carry it back to the barrack room. This procedure was to be repeated every week.

After some tasteless bread and tepid soup, our next introduction to life in the army was a visit to the quartermaster's store to be kitted out with uniform, boots, webbing equipment, blankets, and all the other bits and pieces that form part of a soldier's world. The general rule for fitting uniforms seemed to be: if you could get it on, it would do. This resulted in some very sorry looking soldiers. In time, we learnt to exchange and alter our trousers and tunics until we had some semblance of a uniform that looked, and felt, half reasonable. We were also issued with a *hussuf* — an abbreviation of housewife apparently. This contained needles, thread, and wool, as we had to sew on our own buttons and darn our own socks.

By now we were all exhausted, and collapsed, almost gratefully, into our beds; it had been a long journey, but I had finally made it.

The next day came our induction to army medical care. In the medical room stood the medical officer, or 'MO', and his orderly; the orderly had a list of names, a swab, a dish of spirit, and a tool that we later found out was for inoculating us! The MO had a huge syringe that contained a lurid cocktail of vaccines against all the diseases known to man. The procedure was quick and efficient, but hardly hygienic. First, the orderly gave each man a quick wipe on the arm with his swab, followed by a smart dab with his inoculating tool, which resembled a miniature branding iron. Each man then moved on to the MO and again there was a quick dab with the swab; the huge syringe was inserted into the arm, followed by a squeeze, and another dab with the swab. After all of us had been inoculated, we were sent on our way. The same syringe and needle were used on every man, with the occasional wipe with a swab dipped in spirit. For the next forty-eight hours or so I was quite ill, with swollen arms, fever, and feeling like death, not even warmed up. How anyone survived is a miracle.

Our first parade was taken by the Regimental Sergeant Major, or 'RSM', who introduced himself by saying, "Forget everything you were taught at Sunday School, in this man's army I'm GOD!" And he meant it.

Lectures followed on the history of the regiment, its battle honours, and its Victoria Cross heroes.

At the time, this seemed to be a bit over the top, but in due course the spirit of the regiment was instilled into us and simply became a part of our lives. These inter-regimental rivalries were encouraged by the army in order to foster regimental spirit. This even extended to an orchestrated regular Saturday night scuffle between members of each regiment, resulting in a few bloody noses and cut lips as proud tokens of our willingness to uphold the honour of the regiment.

Members of the battery were drawn from all walks of life and from all parts of the country. Some real characters emerged as the weeks went by and we began to get to know and inevitably become dependent upon each other.

At 7 a.m., the corporals would whisper *sweet-nothings* in our ears:

"Hands off your cocks,
put on your socks,
and get out of bed."

We were soon up, washed and shaved in cold water; our beds were made, blankets folded, and groundsheet kit all neatly stacked and presented for inspection. Some people did not even sleep in their beds; they would rather sleep on the floor than disturb their kit.

At six a.m., the PT Instructor, 'Mister Muscles', would be there jumping us about like demented creatures for thirty minutes before breakfast. After breakfast, the drill sergeants would take over shouting and bellowing. We became very fit and acutely alert very quickly, which stood us in good stead for what was to come.

Pay Parade took place every Friday at 4 p.m., which also coincided with the finish of the weekly cross-country run. Anyone who failed to complete the run or was late back did not get paid until Saturday, which meant missing the Friday night session at the local pub — a very severe punishment!

When you did things wrong, which was often, you were sentenced to *jankers*. This meant having to report to the guardroom every hour on the hour in a different order of dress, which would be decided by the guard commander; this continued until he felt you had been punished enough. If he was not satisfied with the standard of dress, you would be ordered to run around the barrack square, and so the time you had to prepare for the next hourly visit to the guardroom became shorter than ever. Everyone mucked-in to help by getting everything ready for the next visit to the guardroom, which was testimony to the essential comradeship that developed. If you were unlucky to get punishment over weekends, it was spent doing *fatigues* such as cleaning showers and toilets, scrubbing floors, and sweeping the parade ground.

For the next eight weeks, we learnt to march, fire assorted lethal weapons, throw hand grenades, and generally become soldiers. We also had lectures on the effects of mustard gas attacks that were absolutely terrifying because everyone was well aware of the effect it had on soldiers in the First World War.
Discipline, good order, and attention to detail were drummed into us from morning till night, and although at the time we moaned and groaned, I must say that it stood us in good stead during the years that were to follow.

When not in lectures, if we were not marching around the parade square, we ran everywhere, at what they called *double-time*. We learnt combat skills in the training area, which they called *Happy Valley*. The army has a particularly sick sense of humour sometimes! Crawling over the thick undergrowth made our arms and elbows bleed. Climbing trees and crossing rivers hanging from a rope were also unpleasant experiences; simply put, if your hands slipped, you fell in. No matter where you ran, you did so with full equipment and rifles, as well as corporals and sergeants running beside you shouting; "The Germans are good, you've got to be better. The Germans are fast, you've got to be faster. The Germans are strong, you've got to be stronger!"

And so it went on, all day long, until we collapsed on our beds in the evening.

The last week of basic training was *test week*, during which time we were pushed to our very limits. One day, we were required to march a gruelling twenty-five miles in full kit: ammo boots, full webbing, a thirty-pound backpack, and a rifle. Another memorable day found us on the range to test our ability to use the rifle, Bren gun, and other weapons. This was then followed by the dreaded assault course, during which encouragement was sometimes physical as well as verbal. Finally, we were ordered to undertake a forced march of five miles in two hours carrying full battle order, an eight-pound pack, a rifle, and sixty rounds of ammunition.

The passing out parade was held on the final day of the week and my sense of pride in the regiment and my pals was tremendous. Marching past the colonel as he stood on the saluting dais, I felt ten feet tall and fit as a hundred fiddles. Pride does not begin to describe the feeling.

After the parade, we were told which guns we would be trained on next. I was very pleased to learn that I would be specialising in the heavy anti-aircraft guns, or 'HAA', rather than the light anti-aircraft guns, or 'LAA'.

Our reward for all these efforts was a week's home leave. I can recall walking down the lane to my grandparents' home and feeling so proud. It always irked me that my father never once said he was proud of me, but that was the way he was; that was the way most fathers were then.

A standing joke amongst troops at the time was the fact that, every time you went on leave, almost the first things anyone asked were: "How long have you got?", "When are you going back?", and "How many Jerry's have you shot?" This seemed to happen to everyone.

I met up with my old pal Bill Rushton, who had joined up earlier and was on leave, prior to joining his unit in North Africa. We spent our evenings in Stoke–on-Trent, dancing and drinking, and even found time to get a photograph taken together before he left.

I also met my brother Walter; he lived at 3 Sun Street, Quarry Bank, near Cradley Heath. He told me about an incident that happened on the 20th December. On that evening, 200 bombers passed over Quarry Bank en route to Liverpool, and for some unknown reason the Luftwaffe dropped two parachute *A-type luftmines*. These bombs were five feet eight inches long, weighed 1,100 lbs. and had a seventeen-second fuse, which activated after hitting something. They also had an explosive radius of 300 feet. One landed on the clubhouse and the other landed on waste ground at the rear of the local cinema, with the parachute ending up in Walter's back garden. Everyone was evacuated to Colley Lane School whilst the two mines were defused, and he was able to return home at 3 p.m. the next day.

Once we had the passing out ceremony at the end of the basic training period, we had more liberty to leave the camp. However, this came with many hazards, mainly the chance of being caught in *out of bounds bars* and returning back to camp after your pass had run out. Avoiding such situations involved various methods of dodging the Military Police. One method was to persuade someone who had a pass to lead the way to the exit from the station. Whilst his pass was being inspected, everyone made a run for it using every possible exit point over the barrier, and even along the railway track. Other approaches included waiting until their backs were turned and using the field craft the army had so usefully taught us. Most of us would usually get away with it, but those that did get caught were on a charge the next day and lost any hope of getting a genuine pass in the future.

"We were drunk last night,
we were drunk the night before,
we're going to get drunk tonight
if we never get drunk anymore.
The more we drink,
the merrier we shall be,
for we are the boys of the Royal Artillery."

4

Ack-Ack

At its peak during the war, the Anti-Aircraft Command was the largest single organisation in the British Army and served under the command of General Sir Frederick Pile for the entire duration of the war. It is disappointing that, in post-war years the desk-jockeys and publicists of the Air Ministry worked hard to establish the myth that only the RAF's Fighter Command did anything to keep the Luftwaffe out of British skies. The Air Ministry sought to deny the Anti-Aircraft Command much recognition; this is a view which, in their defence, has never been held by RAF aircrews themselves. One of Winston Churchill's most famous speeches, broadcast after the Battle of Britain, told how: "Never before in the field of human conflict was so much owed, by so many, to so few."

I like to think that the *few* consisted of the brave young fighter pilots up there, as well as the *few* of us down on the ground.

At this stage of the war, equipment was in short supply. This was mainly due to the fact that guns, trucks, tanks and ammunition had been left behind on the beaches at Dunkirk during the evacuation. As a result, training was generally curtailed, leaving a lot of time to be spent doing useless tasks just to keep us busy and out of mischief. This was a tedious time, which I found extremely boring.

I soon learnt lots of slang words and military abbreviations for absolutely everything, such as *flak* from the German **Flugzeuga**bwehr**k**anone aircraft defence cannon, and common nicknames for anti-aircraft guns such as 'AA', 'AAA' or 'triple-A', and the most widely used, 'Ack-Ack'; this was the World War I phonetic code for the abbreviation 'AA'.

One of our more useful tasks was the driving course, which was undertaken in a small van-type vehicle based on a normal car. It was bitterly cold, and in those days car heaters were unheard of; driving around the country roads in an unheated car was mind- and body-numbing. This was followed by the driving test, consisting of a half-hour drive along a route we had driven many times, and a short cross-country course, and that was that. As far as I know, no one ever failed.

After the van, we moved on to the three-ton truck, which was even worse. Each truck carried five trainees and the instructor, so whilst one trainee was undergoing instruction in the front, the rest of us sat huddled in the back in the freezing cold. Each session took about six hours to complete, and I have never been so cold before, or since. We were under strict instructions that whenever we stopped the vehicle for a break, we were required to camouflage the vehicles with the camouflage net. This was an incredibly cold and laborious business and in an attempt to avoid it we would try to find a group of trees. However, on the moors, such things were few and far between!

After that, we did basic gunnery instruction where I was taught ballistics and trajectories, which consisted mainly of mathematics. This had always been my weakest subject; how I passed my exam at the end of the course I shall never know.

Then I moved on to join A Battery in Sergeant Street's Section, which contained an interesting mixture of characters. I commenced intensive training, mostly on the beautiful 3.7-inch anti-aircraft gun. It was the primary British heavy anti-aircraft gun; ours was mobile, which meant it could be moved from site to site at great speed.

There were two main types of heavy anti-aircraft gun. Basically, there was the 4.5-inch, which had a short range and a high explosive shell, and the 3.7-inch, which had a greater range or, as they liked to say, a 'higher ceiling'; it also had a faster rate of fire. For high-altitude bombers, you would use the 3.7-inch, and for attacking fighter aircraft you would use the 4.5-inch. Simple!

So how did it all work? A gun section or detachment was normally composed of ten men, and they had to learn every position inside and out. These consisted of:
  'No.1' who was in command of the gun
  'No.2' who adjusted the gun direction
  'No.3' who worked the elevation
  'No.4' who set the dial number on the shell's fuse
  'No.5' who operated the gun's breech
  'No.6' who rammed the shell home
  'No.7' and 'No.8' who were the loaders
  'No.9' who operated the predictor
  'No.10' who supplied the ammunition.

This was the official gun team structure, but we were always told that, "One day you may well find yourself alone but still operating the gun." That was the reason why we had to learn every position.

The predictor was a mechanical machine – perhaps the first ever computer. This computer was fed the basic information from the spotters, regarding height, range and bearing; you added in temperature, air pressure, wind speed and direction, and then calculated the aircrafts' speed and course before predicting where the target would be when a shell arrived. The range was essential for setting the fuse, and because there was no chance of a direct hit on an aircraft, contact fuses were not used. Instead, the shell had a time fuse which needed to be set immediately before firing so that it would explode sufficiently close to the target.

During subsequent weeks, we trained and trained, mastering each different position on the guns. I worked as spotter on the height and range finder, but most importantly on the predictor, which was extremely complicated, although I always enjoyed using it. I remember the first time they took the panel cover off the predictor, we all gasped at the complicated wiring.

"Do we have to learn that?" we echoed.

"No" said the instructor, "but I have to show it to you anyway."

We were on the gun and outside all the time. I remember how cold my hands could get and how they needed to be protected, especially when working instruments. We were issued with special white sheepskin mittens, which had short topless fingers and an ingenious flap that could be fastened back or brought over the finger-ends as necessary.

Although every position on the gun was important, the number nine had the great responsibility of predicting the fuse number and yelling it to the number one, who then gave the order to set the fuse and load the gun, before shouting "FIRE!!"

The number nine also had to allow for the time it took for those three actions. For all this to work, the enemy plane had to remain at a constant speed and on the same course.

At the same time, the number one would be attached, via a field telephone, to the Command Post, receiving the orders and shouting out at us to "search" and "follow" and maybe to "fire."

My favourite was; "stand-down…"

When the guns did go off, if you were spotting you had to hold your nerve, because if you lost sight of the plane or moved the dials, the predictor was starved of the numbers needed to do its job. We were only meant to be spotting for two hours maximum, as after that fatigue set in and accuracy was lost.

I hated being on spotter duty. The only bit I liked was that you got to sit on a swivel chair which, at the time, was a great novelty. When you saw an approaching plane through your binoculars, you checked, then double-checked, the plane recognition pamphlet to see if it was hostile or not. If it was hostile then you sounded the alarm. You then moved over to a Telescope Identification instrument — a fancy telescope we called the 'TI'. It had two eye pieces at either end of a bar, sat on a tripod; you had to keep the plane fixed in the telescope's viewfinder whilst someone else read out the height and bearing from the scale on the base of the telescope and shouted them out to the predictor operator. However, the plane would move in and out of the viewfinder and constant adjustments were needed as the new bearings were shouted out. It was not uncommon, at that stage, for someone to accidentally knock the telescope or walk in front, which would be followed by a colourful and robust exchange of words!

Once we had mastered the gun, we were sent to fire camp. This was where we used live ammunition on live targets. The RAF tow plane would fly the targets across the sky for us to shoot at, which was known as 'pulling my darling'.

Soon, the training was over and I received my orders to join the Sixtieth Field Regiment in Birmingham.

Artillery Evolution
In the Beginning there were foot soldiers, infantry 'grunts';
General Rejects, Unfit for Normal Training.
A small proportion of these grunts were endowed with brain cells and evolved, to be the 'officer-class', known as Rupert's and Rodney's. The R's had a great dislike for wallowing in mud, which is more than an occupational hazard for grunts. So, to escape from the mud, they conquered their fear of heights and mounted horses.
They then trained other grunts to mount these beasts and they became known as Cavalry and the Royal Horse Artillery, or 'Donkey Wallopers'. But, they found that their beasts necessitated too much care and attention. An alternative was needed and it came in the form of machines.

Then came the tank and long-range artillery, which shortened the lives of the grunts and the donkey wallopers considerably. Less not we fear, for they then invented the aeroplane; an airborne machine that could drop from the sky some incredible things, to land on the tank and the long-range artillery.

This is the time in Army evolution, when a most significant metamorphosis occurred. An elite force of courageous men evolved to face the might of this airborne threat.

'THE ANTI-AIRCRAFT GUNNER'

5

The Birmingham Blitz

The Birmingham Blitz began on the 9th August 1940, and ended on the 23rd April 1943. Around 1,800 tons of bombs were dropped, killing 2,241 residents and seriously injuring thousands more with 13,000 buildings destroyed and thousands more damaged. Birmingham was the third most heavily bombed city after London and Liverpool, and had already been subjected to over eight months of bombing when I arrived at my unit on the 28th April 1941.

I was posted to the Second Anti-Aircraft Corp, Eleventh Anti-Aircraft Division, Thirty-fourth Brigade, Sixtieth Field Regiment, and billeted on the recreation field just off Church Road in Yardley; the *Rec* is now called Old Yardley Park.

Two weeks before I arrived, Yardley had been bombed over a two-day period, with at least nine high explosive bombs landing on the town and causing considerable damage. This was still evident as we drove through the town to our camp. They were probably aiming for the battery of 3.7s, as well as the search light and barrage balloon sites on the outskirts of Oaklands Park on the other side of Yardley. Fortunately, they missed!

The camp was quite comfortable; the accommodation consisted of Nissan huts which had been built mostly by Italian prisoners of war. Each hut held ten men and had its own coal fire, which was a real luxury. The huts were arranged in what was known as a 'spider'; more specifically, four huts would all converge on an ablution block which contained our toilets, washbasins, showers and sinks. I think there were at least five 'spiders'. All the paths were lined with white-washed stones, which was not as daft as it sounds, because it made them visible at night. We had a guardroom, cookhouse and a Navy Army Air Force Institution, better known as the 'N.A.A.F.I' hut. There we sat around playing cards, drinking tea, and eating buns; we could also buy our rations of chocolate and cigarettes at the hut, with cigarettes costing around one shilling for twenty.

There was still the constant worry that we would come under attack from German paratroopers. On more than one occasion, incendiaries and mines, which were attached to parachutes and often came down on mass, were mistaken for the enemy and we found ourselves being sent out to engage with Jerry paratroopers.

The other problem was that around one fifth of the high explosive bombs failed to detonate, as did one third of the parachute incendiaries and mines. We would turn-up expecting to encounter Germans, only to be met by suspended bombs with their parachute cords caught in various obstacles such as trees, gently blowing in the breeze with the expectation that they might go bang any second.

My first experience of being bombed was very frightening. I was acting as a spotter, sat in a swivel chair which looked a bit like a wooden deckchair with large arm-rests and grooves to cup your arms in so you could rest them whilst looking through binoculars for long periods at a time. It was great fun spinning around, until you got caught that is. I remember it well; it was just before dusk, with the Battery Sergeant Major shouting out "TAKE POST!"

About thirty minutes later, the sirens sounded and those who could take cover in the air raid shelters did so. This did not include me, as I was spotting. I could hear but not see the aircraft coming directly overhead; I then heard the Detachment Commander order "Engage."

The search light had only just gone on when suddenly I could hear the whistling of a falling bomb, then an explosion which rattled my teeth. By the time the second bomb was on its way down, I was on the deck closer than a cow-pat! There were four bombs, the nearest of which fell about 150 yards away. When I saw the craters the next morning, it did not do much for my morale. No doubt the German pilot thought he had got us, but he was a degree or two out. The only casualty was a dog. There was not a mark on him; instead, he was just lying on his back with his legs sticking straight up, close to one of the craters. It was probably the blast that killed him. Poor thing, I thought; he was not doing any harm.

Normally, every gun section had one evening and one day off each week. This was because of the number of soldiers that were needed to keep a gun ready for action over a twenty-four-hour period. For example, take a half battery with four guns and a nominal strength of around 140 soldiers. At any given time, there would be a full section assigned to each gun, with eight spotters working the height finders. There was also a fire picket, a decontamination squad, stretcher bearers, a medical orderly, the guard, and don't forget a bunch of officers and senior NCOs to run the whole show. Added to this, there would be one section away on courses, another away from camp, guarding other sites or helping with bomb rescue, and yet another section away on leave. Then there were those in hospital or sick, and twenty on their weekly day off. This was why I only got one night off a week.

I loved girls, drinking, fighting, and dancing, in no particular order. At every opportunity, when off duty, we would take the No.15 bus into town to find a place to go dancing; everyone was determined to continue to live life to its fullest, no matter what. I cannot remember its name, but there was a magnificent ballroom in the city centre, with plush seats and two orchestras. When one orchestra was relieved, the stage would slowly revolve, and a fresh orchestra would then appear playing the same tune as the one that was exiting. It was all so well done; we went there a lot. One night we were on the dance floor ignoring the sirens; we could hear the bombs getting closer and the conductor of the orchestra announced that "Everyone should evacuate in an orderly fashion", which we did. Shortly after that, the building was thankfully completely empty, when a parachute mine dropped on the ballroom, and it was blown to smithereens.

On another night out we met a group of girls who were *bargees*. They worked the canal barges between London and Birmingham, transporting up to fifty tons of steel and copper at a time for the Grand Union. The trip took three weeks each way, and they were out for a night on the town, before returning the next day. Prior to the war, this and other jobs were all-male institutions, and girls were rapidly taking the jobs on to free the men for conscription.

On Saturday the 10th May, just after midnight, the air raid sirens sounded; I rushed to my action station, and could see the search light battery to our south in Earlswood searching the sky for enemy aircraft. About ten minutes later, the search lights at Acocks Green, which was around a mile south of us, also came to life, and immediately picked up a lone Heinkel flying very low at about 500 feet, and heading towards us. It quickly passed over our position and appeared to be turning in a westerly direction to carry out what we assumed was a bombing run on the city centre. It was too low for the heavy anti-aircraft guns to engage, so our lights had a go; I grabbed my rifle, and along with everyone else, had a go myself.

The plane was soon gone, but we were able to follow its progress as different crews engaged it. First it headed west for a short while, then south back towards where it had first been spotted; it then appeared to be circling over Hollywood and Earlswood. Being the only plane in the sky, everyone appeared to be having a go at shooting it down, so we weren't surprised when it eventually crashed.

The next morning, we heard that the searchlight battery at Fulford Heath was the installation which had shot it down, and the soldiers there had also taken a prisoner. I had just come off duty and was sitting in the canteen eating breakfast, when a Sergeant came in and told a few of us to get a truck and make our way with him to the crash site to get a souvenir to put on the wall. We made our way to the 380th Searchlight

Battery, which was on open farmland on Fulford Heath. But before we got there, we met some troops a short distance away, who directed us down Rumbush Lane to the wreck, which was in a field belonging to Kidpile Farm. By the time we arrived there was quite a crowd, and the Home Guard had posted sentries to keep everyone away. The Sergeant went to see the duty officer to tell him that we had *also* engaged the aircraft and were responsible for shooting it down and had come to claim our prize!

I don't know exactly how it happened, but a short while later the local newspaper arrived and wanted to take a picture of the aircraft with those who had shot it down. Before I knew it, myself and another of the lads were paraded in front of the plane with a number of other soldiers for a group photograph. The next day the picture was in the Birmingham Daily Mail; our unit never got a mention, and all the credit went to the searchlight crew, which was right since they did actually shoot it down. I think the only reason I got into the picture was because the Sergeant was making so much noise about our involvement, the officer shoved us in just to keep the peace. We never got a souvenir, because the RAF investigators took over – but at least I got my picture in the paper. The big winners were the local women, who were able to salvage the parachutes and made themselves silk knickers.

I found out later that the lone Heinkel had been sent on a secret mission, to drop a 1,000kg and four 250kg bombs on the

Birmabright Aluminium Works at Quinton. To get to the works, the German bomber would have followed navigation points such as rivers, canals, railways and prominent landmarks like reservoirs to aid it in reaching the bombing location. It seemed that the crew became disorientated and were circling around lost, looking to find landmarks, when they were shot down.

The crew of the Heinkel He111H-8 Code G1+MT were:
    Oblt Johann Speck von Sternberg aged twenty-three - Pilot;
    Fw Fritz Muhn aged twenty-four - Observer;
    Fw Siegfried Ruhle aged twenty-one - Flight Engineer;
    Gefr Rudolf Buddle aged twenty-one - Wireless Operator and the only survivor of the crash.

The dead airmen were buried three days later at Robin Hood Cemetery in Hall Green. Their remains were moved to the German War Cemetery at Cannock Chase in 1962.

A week later, on the 17th May, I was with my section in the city, helping to clean up and recover bodies from the bombing the night before, when the bombers came over on a daylight raid. We returned to our camp to find that it had been hit and one of the spiders had been destroyed, killing a couple of gunners who were on their day off. That was not the last time the camp was hit. A few years later, a rocket from Z battery at Swanhurst Park landed on a hut, killing some Auxiliary Territorial Service (ATS) girls.

On another occasion, a bomb hit a viaduct which brought water from the Elan Valley Reservoirs in Wales to Birmingham. This cut off the water supply. All the lakes and canals were drained nearly dry to fill the tenders of the fire engines. It became so bad that Royal Engineers started blowing up certain buildings to create firebreaks because of the fear of firestorms from the extensive bombing.

Our gun-site was quite a distance from the camp at Selly Oak Park — some nine miles away. It was a static site with four guns, searchlights, and barrage balloons. However, this was only a temporary arrangement whilst they built permanent concrete constructions at Swanhurst Park and Edgbaston.

It was not long before we had settled down into a well-drilled team with experience of actual raids. There were loads of false alarms, and we were often ordered *to post* for what turned out to be friendly RAF planes. Added to this, the dynamos on some types of electric trains and trams sounded like distant air-raid sirens, and a motor bike could sound just like the intermittent drone of a plane — similar enough to get someone shouting.

When something happened for real, the first indication came from the observers, who notified us that enemy aircraft were approaching. They called in, "Seen", followed by the chart reference, for example "7756". This would then be followed by the number of planes approaching, for instance "9", and then the height in feet, perhaps "At 10,000", and finally the type of plane — "Heinkel 111", etc.: as a result, an observer cried out, "SEEN, 7756, 9 at 10,000, HEINKEL 111."

This let the spotters know in which direction they should focus their attention. Once the planes were in the telescope viewfinder, they would shout out the bearing and angle. As the planes moved across the sky, they would continue to shout out new reports; it was a breathless but exciting business.

I remember when we shot down our first German plane, a Heinkel 111 bomber, along with other gunners no doubt. I watched it come screaming out of the sky. We looked out for parachutes, but none appeared; then came the crash, quite some distance away, and we saw the black smoke, but no one cheered. I think it was because we were aware that even though it was the enemy, there had been five young men just like ourselves in that plane. Later, my attitude hardened. They were out to destroy my country, family and friends, and I got the greatest satisfaction when all four guns on our site blazed away at them and I felt I was doing something useful.

On occasions when we were at it continuously night and day, our gun barrels became so hot that we had to pour cold water down them; I still remember watching them steam. We heard later that this was not such a good idea!

Between raids, we were told to stand down and return to our dugouts; but on warm dry nights, many of us would lie on the concrete floor beside the guns, using our helmets as pillows, and have a snooze, as we knew there would be another raid and when it came, we would already be at our posts.

On all the occasions I was in action on the guns, I can honestly and truthfully say I never experienced fear. We were so highly trained and at such a pitch that we carried out our duties knowing exactly what we had to do. But that was on the guns. One day, I was out in town on a day off, when the air-raid sirens sounded and everybody in the streets disappeared. I was all alone and lost, with bombers overhead, and then I experienced fear. This was mainly because I did not know where to go or what to do, so I threw myself down in the gutter and stayed there shaking until the all clear sounded. The street was suddenly full of people staring at me sympathetically. I then rushed into the nearest pub and had a stiff drink.

On Sunday mornings, a Padre would turn up from nowhere and lay out his paraphernalia on a trestle table in the middle of the site. We would all have to assemble and listen to him telling us that it was a sin to kill, to love our enemies, and to offer the other cheek when struck. When the alarm sounded, we would all rush helter-skelter to our posts and start firing away, trying to kill enemy aircrew until ordered to cease fire and then stand down. That meant then returning to our *church* where the Padre continued to tell us not to kill and to love our enemy. I then imagined German Padres over there telling their young flock the same thing, and so the war carried on. I wondered who would win this war; those who prayed the hardest, or those who fought the hardest?

In mid-October, I saw a note pinned to the battery notice board asking for volunteers for *special duties*. Normally, it was a golden rule never to volunteer for anything! I don't know why, but on this occasion it seemed it might be a good idea...

"Anybody here know shorthand?" asked the Corporal.
A soldier took one step forward.
"Then get to the cookhouse," he bellowed.
"They're short-handed."

"If in doubt, put down smoke and move left,"
and
"Never volunteer for anything."

6
Carrots

When I arrived for 'special duties' training in Tamworth, I was introduced to what was called Radio Direction Finding ('RDF') equipment. It was not long after that the Yanks came up with the new name, an abbreviation for **RA**dio **D**etection **A**nd **R**anging, or 'RADAR'.

By today's standards, it does not sound particularly impressive, but at the time, radar was one of our country's best kept secret weapons. Such was the secrecy surrounding it, that neither I nor anyone involved could tell a soul how we spent our days — not even those soldiers who worked alongside us. As far as my family and everyone else was concerned, I was still on the guns; no one could be let into the secret. This secret was eventually revealed at the end of the war, when the Air Ministry disclosed the use of radar; although, to be fair, by then, it was not a secret to our troops or our enemies, just the general population. However, it was not until 1991 that the government released us from our Official Secrets Act oath and I was finally allowed to disclose my experiences. As far as I know, every single soul kept their mouths shut throughout the war about what they were doing.

Originally, the development of radar was spurred on by fears that the Germans and Japanese were developing some kind of *death ray*. It sounds crazy, but, at the time we believed in all that science fiction stuff; hand-held ray guns, Flash Gordon, UFOs and the like. What actually happened was that, in trying to develop the death-ray, instead of disintegrating the target, the signal just bounced back; eventually one of the boffins realised that this failure could be used to detect objects instead.

By the start of the war, the technology had got to the stage where it could be used, and the RAF built secret radar sites around the coast, collectively known as the 'Chain Home Network', to detect approaching German aircraft. It certainly saved our bacon when it came to the Battle of Britain in 1940.

The RAF ran the chain network, but the technology was rapidly advancing and was now small enough to be put onto mobile trailers and used in the field; one such application was to support anti-aircraft operations, and that is where I came in.

Keeping a secret is hard enough, but one war-time myth that was actively encouraged was related to vitamin A. Lack of vitamin A can cause poor vision, including night vision, and a good source of this vitamin is carrots; as such, it was made known that eating large quantities of carrots would help you see in the dark. This rumour arose during the Battle of Britain, when the RAF circulated a story about their pilots' carrot consumption, in an attempt to cover up the use of radar technology in engaging with enemy planes. This myth was further developed to include anti-aircraft gunners, to help explain how we were able to shoot down German planes at night!

Before radar, we relied on a thing called *sound location*, which involved someone listening, through a set of large headphones, for the sound of aircraft. Then, by using a stopwatch, it was possible to work out distances and bearings.

Several of these contraptions would be set up about a mile apart, and would give very good positioning information. They continued to operate alongside the radars throughout the war; but they were not just used to detect aircraft, and were often employed to determine enemy artillery locations, and track ships as well as submarines. The big problem with locators was that, because of the speed at which some of the aircraft travelled, they were only able to give a few minutes warning. Regardless, they were still kept in service as a back-up for when the RDF stopped working or was not available.

I was introduced to the GL 1 RDF long wave model. It was all new and shiny, and I think manufactured in Canada; a very reliable set designed for early warning and continuous tracking.

We were instructed by RAF personnel and lecturers from Stafford University. The GL1 was fitted in a steel control cabin which was mounted on a trailer. On the roof was an aerial dish and two, four-foot parabaloid aerials for transmitting and receiving. These aerials needed to be washed and dried, lightly greased and re-set every day. The receiver had four little cathode ray tubes, or, if you like, television screens. They would each tell me the range, the bearing and the height of the approaching aircraft. One of these tubes was particularly small in size and was used for plane identification. All of this needed a high voltage electricity supply, so a Lister generator was mounted onto another trailer, making the whole setup a two-vehicle caravan.

Next, we needed quite a large area of flat, open ground all around the trailers, so that the transmitter and receiver could work. One hour at a time was enough for anyone's eyes and concentration, so being *off the tube* was always welcomed. Worst of all was that miserable feeling around two in the morning, when your body is at its lowest ebb, crying out to be asleep, yet having to force itself to stay awake.

The radar was fantastic. It was 99% bang on every time, and once the Germans got wise to what we had, they tried all sorts of dodging moves, like dropping tinfoil streamers to confuse the readings!

The RAF personnel who operated RDF wore a radio operator's trade badge; the army was slow to adopt theirs, mainly because of the secret nature of the work. Officially, the radar operator badge came into service in 1944, but earlier in 1942 the army introduced an unofficial badge, similar to that worn by the RAF, but on a khaki background.

Once the course ended, I was promoted to Lance Bombardier. I never returned to Birmingham, and instead was given a 72-hour pass with orders to report to the Royal Artillery Headquarters in Woolwich, London, on the 23rd December.

Soon after arriving, I received my movement orders; I was to join the overseas Malaya Command, sailing by convoy from Liverpool to Bangkok, where I would receive further orders to travel on to Singapore by boat or train.

7
All at Sea

Saturday the 10th January 1942 was an icy cold wintry day at Liverpool Docks; heavy snow covered most of the British Isles, and with temperatures well below zero, it was pretty miserable. We had spent the last few nights in a stable block outside the city and arrived very early to catch the midday high tide, so we would be well on our way before nightfall to avoid the evening bombing. We now found ourselves waiting dockside, stamping our feet to keep warm, in readiness to board our troop ship.

The general conversation was about the Japanese Army occupying Manila in the Philippines the previous weekend, and their continued occupation of outlying islands; a little worrying when your destination is Burma. Reports that the *Japs* don't take prisoners were already well-known, and we later heard that all the defenders of Manila had been killed. It would be almost a year later that the Japanese would bomb Pearl Harbour, and the Americans would join the war; until then, it was Britain alone.

Our ship was the RMS Otranto. She was built in 1929 by Vickers Armstrong at the Barrow in Furness Yard and was a passenger ship for the Orient Line's service sailing from the UK to Australia. At the outbreak of the war, the SS Otranto was lying off Port Moresby, New Guinea, when she was ordered back to Sydney, Australia, where all passengers disembarked. The ship was then requisitioned as a troop ship, painted a drab battleship grey, and mounted with weapons before sailing to Britain. The ship had two funnels, but one was a cosmetic addition, to make the passenger liner appear grander than it actually was, and on this, a machine-gun was mounted. She survived the war, and in 1949 resumed passenger service on the London to Sydney route until 1957, when she was scrapped at Faslane, Scotland.

This was the closest most of us had ever been to anything larger than a pleasure steamer. In her happier days as a cruise liner she would have been more glamorous than we ever knew her. There were no fancy brochures, or even a return date, and so began my wartime 14,000-mile cruise.

I boarded the ship, my world in two kit bags and my rifle slung over my shoulder. All *other ranks* were issued with a hammock, two blankets, and a lifejacket, then crammed into the bowels of the ship and basically told to "Get on with it!" Officers faired a little better, with subalterns sharing a cabin and captains and above having their own.

It took all morning to load the ship, and soon after noon we left our mooring. We were wrapped up to the eyeballs in greatcoats and scarves to keep out the icy blasts. Snow fell like a huge white blanket, as most of the whole draft, some 2,000 souls, including nurses and Women's Auxiliary Air Force (WAFS), stood on deck looking portside, watching the shore and the Liver Building receding into the distance.

We were well on our way, when the air-raid sirens sounded and Liverpool responded, as it had so many times before to its unwelcome visitors. Bombs fell near to the cathedral, and although they did not know it, that night would be the last raid on Liverpool.

The following day we were in the Clyde, and on the Monday we joined our convoy off Oversay, the Orset islet. We joined other ships to form the Winston Special convoy No.15, or WS 15. Our ship was labelled 22L, which became our oceanographic address and floating reference point.

In June 1940, France had surrendered to Germany, and with the invasion of Britain anticipated, it was an act of considerable faith that Britain sent forces to Africa, rather than bolstering British defences. The reason for this decision was that Egypt and East Africa had only limited garrisons and the threat of losing the Suez Canal was real. Added to this, the loss of the oil resources of Iraq and Persia would also have been devastating. To protect these vital resources, it became necessary to reinforce the Egyptian garrison by sea. Unfortunately, this could only be achieved by going via South Africa. This would be the case until 1943, when the Mediterranean became safe for allied shipping. These routes to the east became known as *Winston Specials*, so named because the first convoy was organised on the express orders of the Prime Minister.

A famous young Midshipman sailed with WS01, known to the Gunroom as "Phil the Greek"; more properly he was known as Midshipman, Prince Philip of the Hellenes, now HRH Prince Philip, Duke of Edinburgh.

These convoys were not simply transporting soldiers; each WS convoy exhibited a complete military formation of many thousands of troops, plus their personal baggage and equipment, stores, transport, artillery, armour and so on. The entire force, on arrival, formed a complete fighting unit at a Divisional level.

The first leg of the voyage took us deep into the Atlantic Ocean, and for three days the convoy battled storms of force 8 to 10, with mountainous seas and strong winds. On board, virtually everyone was seasick for days; the only relief came from staying on deck as long as possible. Down in the galley stood a large barrel labelled *Ship's Biscuits for Sea-Sick Soldiers*. This barrel contained large square biscuits rather like dog biscuits — hard as rocks; if they could be stomached they certainly helped overcome the perpetual feeling of wanting to vomit at every lurch of the ship. This was not helped by the fact that the ship had a flat bottom, a design feature which enabled it to navigate into thousands of small outposts of the Empire. However, it was not great at cutting through large waves. It took time, but I eventually learned the rhythm of the sea and got my *sea legs*.

I spent as much time *up top* during the day as I could, slipping and sliding around on the icy deck. I shivered into my greatcoat and gazed inevitably out to sea to realise that I was not alone — this was a convoy. Eventually, the convoy turned south and the storms abated, with the temperatures rising to more comfortable levels.

It did not take long for some pioneers to discover that each lifeboat contained an emergency ration of rum, which they proceeded to steal!

A restrictive military and very boring daily routine was soon adopted; it started with the Captain's Inspection, whilst standing at morning boat stations and listening to cries of "Tighten that life jacket or you'll break your ruddy neck when you hit the water!"

Later, we would sit facing outward and stare at the sea, or read, play cards or talk, before going below for lunch. At meal times, we would file in and sit ourselves along the mess tables, crammed into groups of twenty. The two people sitting at the end were the only ones able to move around and had the privilege of being the galley slaves, collecting our food and drink. One thing I should mention about life on board a troopship is the bread. This was baked fresh on board each day and was far and away the best bread I think I have ever tasted.

At night, the bedding storage bunks were emptied and the wise few claimed them for bed spaces. Alternatively, there were the tables; otherwise, you would have to sling your hammock. To *sling a hammock* is the nautical term for the operation. The ropes were tied to appropriate bars and the life jackets, from which I was never parted for the duration of the voyage, were wedged into the end strings as a pillow. Blankets were draped onto the canvas pouch, and at this point it was wise to pause and consider the next step, or rather, the leap. There was the gentle, nonchalant approach, with a carefree whistle on one's lips, or the gymnastic approach, consisting of "One, two, hup!" However, the latter approach was often followed by a "Three, four, down," and a smart return to deck level, complete with bedding. The nonchalant types, already cocooned and watching the antics of others in smug self-satisfaction, would lie there hoping that their rope knots would not slip. Eventually, thumps and curses would die away and sleep would take over, with bodies gently swinging to the rhythm of the sea.

The biggest threat after the ship's food was German U-boats, which had been attacking British convoys with almost complete impunity. The prospect of death in the cold waters, reports of twenty submarines operating in the Atlantic, and our convoy steaming into the thick of it, gave everyone plenty to think about. The continuous strains of playing hide and seek, along with the ramifications of being found, only added to the pressure.

There were unseen sailors whose heavy responsibility it was to listen, guide and search across the treacherous ocean. Lifeboat stations were taken daily, and action stations drills called periodically, when Royal Navy ships sped with purposeful intent across and around the plodding convoy. We did not know if a U-boat was lurking. Below decks, we had briefly checked the odds if a torpedo should strike, and then we swiftly talked of other things.

The U-boats operated in groups known as 'wolf packs'; they were supported in the air by the Focke-Wulf Fw 200, Condor aircraft, which aided in finding allied ships. Through the winter of 1941, the U-boats enjoyed tremendous success and inflicted heavy losses on allied shipping. As a result, 1941 became known as the *Happy Time* among the U-boat crews.

On the day of the 15th January, as we sailed past the Bay of Biscay, an Italian marked Focke-Wulf was seen following and observing the convoy. The message from the sailors was "Give it twenty-four hours and they will be on us."

Sure enough, a submarine attack took place on the 16th, and the RMS 'Llangibby Castle' was hit by a torpedo from a U-402-type Viic. Damaged, but not sunk, she was retired to Ponta Delgada from where, under escort and accompanied by a tug, she returned to Gibraltar and then back to Blighty for repairs.

As for submarine U-402; she was sunk on the 13th October 1943, by an American 'Wildcat' aircraft. She sank somewhere in the middle of the North Atlantic with the loss of all fifty of her crew.

Nine agonising days later, our sailing pattern changed; there was a buzz in the air and word was that we were about to enter a port. Eventually, with our speed decreasing, it became evident that we were running down a channel. There was great excitement on board as land appeared and then the port of Freetown came into focus, giving us our first glimpse of Africa.

The convoy arrived in Freetown on the 25th October, where the *shorter-legged* Atlantic liners and the coal burners required fuel. The whole convoy needed water, and there was no fresh food left. The enormous demand on the limited resources of Freetown was a major problem, leading both to delays in the troop convoys and in the homeward-bound trade convoys moving on. This was mainly caused by the heavy demands on labour aboard the coaling ships, and by the depletion of coal stocks, which were, of course, shipped out from Britain. Water supplies were also a problem, in that Freetown, while certainly not bereft of rainfall, possessed only minimal reservoir capacity, which was very easily overwhelmed by large demands. Ultimately, Freetown was simply an anchorage where all supplies had to be loaded by hand from dockside, or by water boats, which were also in short supply.

Freetown was a very welcome sight after the torments of the previous weeks, and although we were not allowed ashore, the portholes were opened for the first time, which was a welcome joy in view of the heat. We purchased fruit from dockside vendors; this made a very pleasant change, as fruit such as oranges and grapes had not been available back home since 1939.

After a four-day stop, we departed from Freetown on the 29th October, heading out again into the South Atlantic. Some jokers on board hinted at U-boats waiting to pounce, but we left without incident, and I soon relaxed mentally and speculated about crossing the equator.

Within a few days, there was an outbreak of Meningitis, and we were all moved onto the decks for two days whilst the lower quarters were disinfected.

One novelty, if not a luxury, was a seawater shower using special seawater soap, which was unfortunately non-effective. In these restricted conditions, certain social events still took place; alas, not dances or dinners, but talks, lectures and even a boxing tournament. Various talents came to light, and before long, one comedian impersonator announced that he was Bob 'Cape of Good' Hope — a not too subtle clue to our navigational whereabouts.

Our next call was South Africa. Here again, the size of the convoys caused problems, as neither Cape Town nor Durban could accommodate the whole convoy; as such, we had to be divided between the two ports.

We departed with our formation unchanged, escorted by the battleship 'Resolution', and arrived off the Port of Cape Town on the 9th February. Our ship was among the unlucky ones which were ordered on to Durban, where we would arrive on the 13th.

To get to Durban, we would need to sail around the Cape of Good Hope. We sailed through a storm for two days; unbelievable mountainous waves crashed against the side of the ship. It felt, at times, that the rivets holding the ship together would just not hold any longer. There was ice and snow in sixteen-inch-thick sheets across the decks, making movement above deck impossible. Whenever they could, sailors used steam hoses to clear ice so we could move around. The storm remained trapped in my memory for many years, as did the wailing of the other passengers; we were all battened-down, with every sea door secure and made water tight. As quick as it had started, the storm passed, to the relief of everyone on board.

I remember *Lilliburlero*, the signature tune of the BBC Overseas Service that preceded the news bulletins broadcast over the ship's tannoy. One night in early February, we listened to one of Churchill's famous pep speeches, 'Give us the tools'. His voice ebbed and flowed like the sea upon which we sailed, the hiss of the waves being broken by the steel of the bow.

As we entered Durban harbour and lined the landward rails, which saw the famous 'Lady in White', a woman called Perla Siedle Gibson, clad in her trademark white dress and red hat, singing to us through a megaphone from the deck of a torpedoed and half-sunk ship near the mouth of the harbour. She was a well-known local figure, and was married to an Air Sergeant called Jack Gibson, who was serving in Italy. She would drive down from her home on the Berea Road to the harbour entrance as soon as she could see that ships were moving. It was said that she even sang on the day she received news that her son Roy had been killed.

Perla sang to more than 5,000 ships and a total of *about a quarter of a* million allied servicemen and *women; she died in 1971, shortly before her 83rd birthday. A bronze plaque donated by the Royal Navy was erected in her memory on Durban's North Pier on the spot where she used to sing and, in 1995, Queen Elizabeth II unveiled a memorial statue near the Ocean Terminal in Durban harbour.*

We finally stepped onto dry land in Durban, which was bright and sparkling after the drab wartime Britain we had left a month earlier. We tied up alongside the quay, which was filled with cheering men, women and children, and I remember thinking how great it was to be back on terra firma again. We disembarked with one week's shore leave, wearing ridiculously long shorts and hiding our embarrassment beneath enormous sun helmets. Some of the men found themselves billeted at Clairwood Camp, formerly the Imperial Forces Trans-shipment Camp. This was a huge tented village overlooking Clairwood Racecourse, where most of the forces passing through Durban stayed.

Those who were less fortunate and had fallen ill during the voyage never had the chance to benefit from the sunshine, as they were despatched back to Britain on a returning ship.

I had the good fortune of being friends with Sydney Isaac 'Jew Boy' Leventhal; he had relatives living five miles outside the city, and I was invited to tag along. We were ordered to report to the General Office every morning, but other than that our time was our own. We soon found ourselves in a large imposing residence with a lawn the size of a regiment parade square. As we entered the grounds of the mansion, we were waved at by a couple of African women who were sweeping the drive. It didn't look dirty to me, but they kept sweeping it anyway.

We walked everywhere most of the time, but occasionally we had the use of a gigantic American Chrysler Freedom car. We were invited out to parties every night and, in some cases, the female population came to blows over who *owned* who!

Two days after landing, we heard the news that the *Japs* had taken Singapore. If I had been on the previous convoy God knows what dreaded fate would have awaited me at the hands of the Japanese. One thing was clear, my destination and my orders were going to change.

8
Suez

One week's leave changed to four days, and on the 17th February we were back on board the ship; we rendezvoused with a number of ships off the port of Durban to form a new convoy, which was split into three Divisions. From Durban, the normal pattern was for ships to proceed northward to the latitude of Mombasa. Here they would divide into the Bombay ships steaming east, and the Suez contingent going north to Perim or Aden, where the convoy would disperse and proceed through the Red Sea to Suez independently.

Due to the fall of Singapore, the pressure on Indonesian ports meant that they were unable to take any more refugee ships. Along with the danger from Japanese submarines, the Indian sea was starting to become a very cramped and dangerous space, with many escaping vessels making for Bombay.

We returned to a ship that had been scrubbed and fumigated from bow to stern. It stank, but was no longer full of rats, bed-bugs and cockroaches.

I look back with great fondness at my time in Durban, enjoying all the bright lights after *blacked-out Britain*. There was ample food available in the restaurants, and swimming in the ocean, although in restricted areas only, due to the risk of sharks. Of course, there was also the shopping and riding in rickshaws pulled by giant Zulus, the general hospitality, the night clubs, and the girls. As we sailed away to the sounds of the *lady in white*, I said that one day I would go back to Durban, but I never did.

This time our convoy was WS 15A, and once we were on our way, we received amended orders that we were to sail north and bolster the Middle Eastern command in North Africa. This came as an immense relief to all on board, as Malaya was a very unattractive proposition. I was told that our final destination would be Cyprus via Port Said, where we would change ships for the onward journey.

As the ship made slow progress northwards, the temperature rose, but more significantly, so did the humidity. It soon became unbearable to sleep below deck, so many of us took to sleeping on the open deck at night under the stars.

Cleaning the open decks was the province of the *Lascar* seamen, who took great delight in hosing down the decks on which we slept at 5 a.m. in the morning; they would soak any man who was not quick enough to get to his feet, pick up his bedding, and make a run for it.

We had an uneventful voyage, and on the 1st of March, we arrived just off Aden, where we dispersed to proceed independently up through the Red Sea towards Suez.

Sailing the length of the Red Sea was a rather anxious time, because the German Air Force was still very active in the area. Because of this, it was 'full steam ahead' with barrage balloons aloft. It was a magnificent sight; ships in file as far as the eye could see, travelling both ways. Fortunately, the RAF had established airfields in North Africa and was able to provide cover when required. There were also naval ships cruising throughout the sea and providing additional protection, and so this leg of the journey was thankfully quiet.

One of the escort ships was the HMS Centurion; she saw active service in WW1 and had been decommissioned in 1924. However, in 1940, she was reactivated after being fitted with a false superstructure to make her look like the battleship HMS Anson. This was done in an effort to confuse German intelligence, and she patrolled the Red Sea, providing anti-aircraft protection for convoys moving through the area. Every Sunday, she would sail alongside ships, and her band would play popular tunes of the day to very loud applause!

Our next port of call was Suez, at the head of the Suez Canal. Most of us had never been out of the country before, so the sights and sounds of Suez were amazing. Bumboats by the hundreds came alongside, selling everything: fruit, leather goods, watches, and sometimes people's daughters. Each vendor would throw two lines on board — one to haul the goods up, and the other to lower the money down. If anybody tried to cheat by hauling the money back at the same time as hauling the goods back, a tug-of-war would take place with much shouting and swearing on both sides. Usually, the matter would be settled amicably. However, on occasion the lines would be cut, the goods returned to the bumboat, and the money returned to the ship, with comments being made about the parentage of the participants.

Another activity involved the local kids, who would dive for coins thrown overboard from the ship. The clear water meant that the kids could be seen diving in after the coins, coming up with a big smile, and asking for more. Since we only had English coins they probably passed them on to a moneylender at about a tenth of their value.

Travelling along the Suez Canal must be one of the highlights of a modern cruise, but I am afraid it bored me to tears; nothing but desert for mile upon mile. It has always been a regret of mine that I did not have enough knowledge and awareness of history to fully appreciate the experience of travelling through one of the world's most exciting engineering projects. My time during this journey was taken up almost entirely by sleeping, eating and playing cards.

The ship eventually arrived in Port Said, the most godforsaken spot on earth. It was just a watering and fuelling depot: hot, dry, dusty and smelly, with nothing going for it as far as I could see. We spent our last night on board the ship that had been our home for the last three months. The next morning, disembarkation began with the WAFS and nurses going off first, accompanied by good-natured shouts from all of us as we lined the decks; we had got to know them very well, and it was sad to see them leaving.

We were the next to step ashore, laden down with equipment and kit bags. It became an organised stagger through the port, rather than a smart military march to the other end of the harbour, where we boarded trucks which took us to a holding camp a few miles away.

We were accommodated in large bell tents about eighteen feet in diameter. These were erected around a central pole; the men slept with their feet towards the pole, and their heads against the outer wall of the tent. Each tent contained up to twelve men, and all their equipment. Daytime temperatures were in the region of 85°C, but inside the tents, temperatures soared above this, causing sweat to pour from the skin in torrents. Soon, almost everyone was suffering from prickly heat. This was a rash of tiny little pimples that could appear all over the body. It itched and burned like hot needles. At the time, no treatment for this condition existed, except to shower as often as possible.

This was a holding camp, and whilst we waited for our orders, the general rule that soldiers are not allowed to be idle in the British Army was observed. Our days consisted of *discipline at war stations* training, and endless parades that brought gales of laughter to the onlooking old soldiers who made up the permanent staff! We wore pre-war khaki drill shorts known as *Bombay bloomers*, shirts and pith helmets. The shorts were long and wide-legged, and with our lily-white legs we looked an awful sight, very much like the characters in 'It Ain't Half Hot Mom'! By-standers would yell out, "Get your knees brown!" This was much to our embarrassment, as it was a derogative term used for soldiers who had just arrived in-country and with no experience. Anyway if we weren't marching up and down, then we were at the docks offloading supplies.

Then there were the flies. With both armies depositing hundreds of tons of human waste, rubbish, and dead bodies, it was not surprising that there was an infestation of these horrible insects, which fed on the filth, bred in their millions, and spread disease. A small scratch would quickly become infected by the flies, developing into a *desert sore*, which often ulcerated. The simple pleasure of having a brew involved having to constantly keep your hand over the cup and sip through your thumb and finger, otherwise they would be lining up on the rim to take a dive in! You would spend all the time waving your hands around to clear them away — a habit that, after leaving the desert, would continue for some time; it did not matter how far you went into the desert, the flies followed.

On the 1st April, I received movement orders; I was to join the Second Regiment, Twentieth Heavy Anti-Aircraft Battery in Cyprus. Suddenly things started to look up. The next day I was allocated to a passenger boat which took me to Famagusta in Cyprus, where I arrived on the 4th of April.

Shortly after landing I received my orders; I would be attached to the Second Royal Horse Artillery Regiment, which was a regular army unit. I was told that we would be on the move again before the end of the month. My brief time in Cyprus was split between the anti-aircraft positions protecting the Famagusta harbour, and helping dockside, loading and unloading ships. We always knew the fun was about to start when German spotter planes appeared overhead, surveying and photographing the port facilities and our gun sites. We were soon in action trying to scare them off — all good fun!

Nothing serious happened the first week. A few planes came over, one of which did drop some bombs. However, the bombs missed their target and instead destroyed our local pub, which caused great consternation.

The following week, whilst I was working dockside, the Italians came over at about 20,000 feet; this was too high for anti-aircraft, and with no RAF cover, they bombed us. Luckily, there were only a few wounded and nobody killed.

On another day, a German U-boat appeared in the harbour to everyone's disbelief! It was pandemonium as we tried to lower our guns to engage the submarine. To get the correct elevation into the harbour, sandbags and bunker emplacements were pushed aside. It was already on its way when all hell let loose; it scarpered unscathed and we all cheered and laughed so much it hurt.

Over those few weeks I got to know my new outfit; they had been evacuated from Dunkirk, and the previous year were involved in the Battle of Greece; they had been reorganising and refitting in Cyprus ever since. Among our number were old soldiers who had served in Egypt before the war. We would all listen with great interest to their stories; they warned us about the perils that awaited the unwary, particularly as regards local women and the terrible consequences of dallying with the local prostitutes. They also taught us the appropriate technique for dealing with vendors, which mainly involved swearing at them in Arabic. However, the most commonly-used foreign language was English.

On the 21st April, we received new orders; we would be attached to the Twenty-second Guards Brigade under the command of the Second South African Division. Later, on the 28th April, we said farewell to Cyprus and left Famagusta harbour on board a Canadian ferry, for our voyage to Port Alexandria in Egypt, arriving in 'Alex' the following day.

"Why are we waiting?"
"We're waiting for the tide"
"Best news I've heard"
"Why"
"The Meds, tide-less!"

9
Desert Warfare

Now would be a good time to tell you a little about the North African desert, and what I was doing there. It's true to say that the whole of my desert war was characterised by short bursts of violent action, followed by long periods of relative calm, as we and the enemy rebuilt our forces in preparation for the next round of fighting.

Thankfully, whilst in the Port Said holding camp, I had received training, which helped me to acclimatise and aided me in familiarising myself with the techniques of daily living and how to survive in the harsh desert environment.

The character of desert warfare owes much to the geography and the extremes of the climate. The desert was covered in large areas of hard and level ground. However, there were also many topographical features which inhibited military movement, including soft sand *seas* with ever-shifting dunes. Other hindrances included steep-sided dry watercourses called wadis, treacherous salt flats, bolder fields, and ancient sea cliffs, which had become escarpments.

The winter and summer seasons arrived around the same time as they did at home, the difference being the climate. In high summer, the noon temperatures exceeded 40°C, distorting your vision with a shimmering heat haze. Winds were light and the thermals created slender sand columns, known as dust devils, which turned slowly in eerie silence before collapsing. In winter, the climate was mild during the day, similar to a hot summer's day in England; after sunset, however, the temperature plummeted and before dawn reached a point well below zero. Winter was the season of dust storms; howling winds filled the air with sharp flying sand that penetrated the eyes, nose, mouth and clothes. It got into every crack and crevice of my equipment, no matter what precautions I took. Some of these storms were of such severity that they blocked the light of the sun for hours at a time.

The majority of desert wars in the past had been fought in the areas of desert that lay close to water supplies, for obvious reasons. A mechanised army changed this, and took the fighting further afield. However, this meant that the need for fuel was often greater than that of water.

As for movement, apart from the coastal road, which was tarmac, we drove along desert tracks, on compass bearings and even by the stars across the open expanse. The lack of road networks and the distance that needed to be covered were problems for us and the enemy, as we both had to move supplies by truck, with conveys vulnerable to air attack.

The other big challenge occurred as the Army advanced. Supply lines grew longer, which meant troops and equipment eventually became exhausted if supplies were unable to get through. One tactic was to capture enemy supply dumps, so the advance could be sustained. However, this process operated in reverse as troops fell back; they grew stronger as they moved back towards supply dumps, home bases and reinforcements.

In June 1940, Italy declared war on Britain. At the time, they controlled Libya and we controlled Egypt, which included the vital Suez Canal. Within days, British units crossed the border into Libya and captured the Italian Fort Capuzzo. The Italians mounted a counter offensive into Egypt, but were stopped at Sidi Barrani, and in December we attacked again in an offensive called *Operation Compass*. This resulted in the destruction of Italy's Tenth Army, by the British Eighth Army, which then advanced rapidly through Tabruk to and El Agheilar, which is halfway to Tripoli.

Hitler saw the need to bolster the Italian forces to prevent a complete defeat in North Africa. He dispatched the German Afrikakorps under the command of Lieutenant General Erwin Rommel, who became known by his nickname, *The Desert Fox*.

The inevitable happened, and we exhausted our supplies; the Germans and Italians then quickly rolled us back to Tabruk, which was left as a fortress behind enemy lines. It was the Australians who held the city and harbour at Tabruk. The siege lasted for nine months, from April 1941, through to November. Rommel needed Tabruk, because without it he was forced to transport his supplies the 930 miles over land from Tripoli. He failed and the siege was broken; the garrison were relieved by the Allied Eighth Army during *'Operation Crusader'*. The Nazi propaganda called the tenacious defenders of Tabruk *Desert Rats*.

All that racing backwards and forwards along the coast became known affectionately by many names, such as the Stakes, the Musus Gallop, and the Agedabia Handicap. The name depended on which phase of the campaign you were in.

After the siege failed, Rommel withdrew to the west to resupply and prepare for the next fight. In preparation, we readied a defensive line to the west of Tabruk at a place a called Gazala going southwards; this became known as the Gazala Line, and consisted of barbed wire, minefields, and a number of irregularly-spaced strong points or *boxes* linked by deep minefields.

The *box* was originally designed to protect infantry in an established position; they were a kind of rapid makeshift camp. Barbed wire would be placed all the way around the outside, then minefields; there was also a gap, similar to a drawbridge, for getting in and out. At night, the gap would be closed and mines planted. At dawn, *Stand-to* the mines would be taken up. The boxes nearest to the enemy were held by infantry, while those further back served as reserve static positions and as bases from which the armour could operate. The chief *box*, known as Knightsbridge, was around a junction of tracks which supplied the front.

When used to protect a camp, the system worked well. But they were now being used as defensive positions, which was not what they were designed for; *boxes* became independent and unable to help one another if needed.

It was at this point in the conflict that I arrived at the Port of Alexandria.

WHAT IS A DESERT RAT?
In the style of Rudyard Kipling's IF –

IF - you can keep your kit when all around you
are losing theirs and blaming it on you.
If you can scrounge a fag when all refuse you,
But make allowances for their doubtful view.
If you can wait and never tire of waiting,
When there is pushing, let no man push you back.

IF - you can force your heart, nerve and sinew,
To serve on guard, when you should be relieved,
And swear like 'L' with all the breath that's in you,
With all the curses ever man conceived.
If you can make one heap of all your winnings
And scamper just before you start to lose.

IF - you can face the other fellows chinning
And turn deaf ears to their unleashed abuse.
If you can drink and not make it your master,
And leave the thinking to the 'Old C.O'.
If you can meet with 'dear old Lady Astor',
And treat her just though you didn't know.

IF - you can walk with blonds and keep your virtue,
Ride on trams and keep your pay-book safe.
If - Jerry's guns and Eyetie bombs don't fret you,
If you know how to find your way through a Jerry
minefield,
And can spot a Jerry Stuka, and not be some dumb
'onlooker'.

IF - you can trudge for miles on desert roads,
With painful blisters on tired feet, waste no time
debating,

69

But force a British grin and hump your pack.
If you know how to treat a real Kamsin,
And use the sand to keep things clean,
Then yours is the 'blue' my son, and all that's in it.

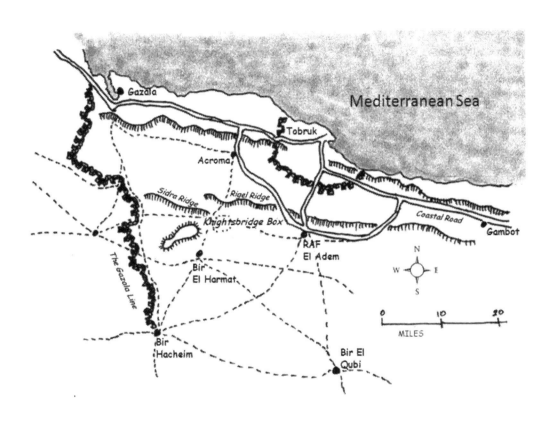

10

The Battle of Gazala
26th May to 21st June 1942

May 1st

The first week in May was taken up by lots of parades. At first, we had a visit from HRH the Duke of Gloucester, then the Army Commander, and to finish off, King George of the Hellenes, who came to thank the troops for their role in the Battle for Greece.

But more importantly, the Royal Horse Artillery holds a 'Drivers Day' celebration every year, to commemorate the actions of the Bull Troops at the battle of Fuentes D'onor in 1811. This event is normally held on the 5th May, but this year, because of all the visits, it was postponed until the 10th. I joined the regimental festivities in Alexandria and, with many others, drank too much beer. As a result, in the early hours, I and others got caught in one of the *out of bounds* bars by the Military Police. The following day, and still very much hungover, I was marched in front of the Commanding Officer, Lt. Col. Bolton, and received a fine of ten days' pay. Not the best first impression to make on my new boss.

May 12th

As there was no radar equipment available, I was allocated to a 4.5-inch anti-aircraft gun crew and we deployed alongside the other heavy artillery guns in the battery. My vehicle was an eight-ton Matador truck. We attached the gun quad to the back, and all twelve of us, along with ammunition and supplies, were crammed into the rear of the truck. We were initially issued with two four-gallon water cans; I grabbed some empty ones from a large stack, filled them up, and stored them on the gun quad. I didn't know it at the time, but this extra water would save our lives later.

May 13th

The day was spent loading vehicles and equipment onto flatbed carriages at Alexandria's railway station. At the end of the day, we set off from Egypt through the night to the railway station at Sollum, which is at the border into Libya, or *Cyrenacia* as it was called then. After offloading, we were caught in a bad sand storm, which delayed our movement. Eventually, we headed east to the regimental forming-up point at the base of a 600-foot escarpment. There was only one road in and out of Libya at this point, through Halfaya Pass, known locally as *Akabah el-Kebir*, the 'great ascent'; I got to know it by another name — *Hellfire Pass.*

May 15th

We received orders to move into the desert and, in the searing heat, reached Bir Hafid the following evening. Thankfully, we made it through the pass without incident.

The next day, we moved again, stopping for the night about seven miles south west of the RAF airfield at El Adem. That evening, Colonel Bolton went on a mission to find an area suitable for a *defensive box*. This search was concentrated about thirty-five miles south west of Tabruk, in an area codenamed 'Knightsbridge'.

May 19th

At first light, we moved into our 'box' area and, with the help of a bulldozer, started to dig defensive positions. We were now in the *Knightsbridge Box*. Why it was given this name, I will never know. As far as I could see, there was no bridge and no box; just a nondescript crossing, with more and more rocky desert. Over the next few days we were joined in the box by some LAAs and the 201st Guards Brigade.

There was no cookhouse and we were told by the Sergeant Major, "You will be cooking your own meals from now on lads." This was called 'truck cooking', and thankfully it had been the method back at the holding camp at Port Said.

We were issued with one week's rations and had to work out what we could eat each day; this meant counting out how many biscuits we could have with each meal. We were also supplied with margarine, jam, bacon, milk, tea, and some tins of fruit, not forgetting the bully beef. To cook my food, I would fill an empty ammunition box with sand and then pour in petrol. Once lit, it would burn for around an hour.

May 22nd

Between stints on anti-aircraft watch and spotter duty, I helped dig trenches and lay minefields along the northern and north east faces of the box.

A convoy arrived late in the afternoon with petrol and water, but with only four days' rations.

The digging, laying midfields and building our defensive positions continued over the next few days. On the 25th, the box was bombed and machine-gunned for ten hours; this started at 9 p.m. and ended at approximately 7 a.m. We were very lucky, as no one in the battery was hurt and no real damage was done. I had spent a sleepless night in my trench, not wanting to get out because of the fear of another attack.

That night, I made out my will on page eighteen of my service and pay book, said my prayers, and tried, unsuccessfully, to sleep.

By the 26th we had still not completed all the defensive positions. More ammunition, petrol and rations arrived, and the Order of the Day warned that the "Huns would attack."

May 27th

At first light, Jerry attacked the Seventh Armoured Division around Bir Hacheim to our south in a mobile tank assault. The Twenty-second Armoured Brigade and Seventh Armoured Division were involved in heavy fighting around Acroma to our north, whilst we sat in the middle waiting for the inevitable to happen.

Then, out of nowhere, the colonel's armoured car came travelling at high speed in my direction. The car then turned parallel to the guns and the colonel, hanging out of the vehicle, yelled "Tank alert! Independent Gunfire! Zero elevation!"

Simply put, this meant each gun for itself.

Shortly after, at around 10 a.m., German tanks arrived at the south west corner of the box. I soon noticed, with mixed horror and interest them getting into position. Then, almost at once, they opened fire on our gun positions. The battery instantly turned its guns around and returned fire. I found myself in the middle of this duel, very exposed and scared. My position received two direct hits. Thankfully, I was in my trench at the time, and was unhurt, but shrapnel had torn through my vehicle.

We knocked out several German tanks before they moved northwards, to be joined by their infantry in an area known as Rigel Ridge. We took some pot-shots at them, but there was now a shortage of ammunition, so it was a limited engagement.

During the day, the Quartermaster took my Lee-Enfield rifle away and issued me with a Thompson sub-machine-gun. This weapon was much better for close quarter fighting, which was what we were now expecting!

That evening, they attacked again, this time the north-west corner, and Lieutenant Norris was wounded and evacuated. In the half light, I watched tracer shells from both sides, innumerable red balls, cruising almost lazily backwards and forwards between us and the escarpment, with the occasional rain of sparks as they ricocheted off the rocks.

I had another sleepless night in my trench and we were getting very low on food, water and ammunition.

May 28th

The Germans were still on Rigel Ridge, and so we intermittently shelled them during the day and they continued to shell us back, with nasty *airburst* artillery fire and machine-guns. Things were starting to get very uncomfortable; we were now almost out of ammunition, and General Ritchie had refused to send additional tanks to our aid. This was because Rommel had put in a diversionary attack near the coast two days earlier. Ritchie believed that this was where the main attack would come, and sent our supplies and reinforcements north; this left us and the southern end of the Gazala Line very vulnerable.

May 30th

During the day, the enemy showed signs of thinning out. We even thought they were withdrawing, as they were seen moving through a gap in the Gazala minefield, after a heavy engagement with the Fiftieth Division. That evening, elements of the battery were ordered to move with a company of Scots Guards and one of the LAA Troops to the west. They were tasked with moving into a position where they could shell the gap in the minefield if needed. However, the column ran slap into the enemy about eight miles west of the box. Where previously we had thought they had withdrawn completely, they had in fact left a strong rear-guard, which our boys ran straight into. It was a disaster; over 100 men went missing, and thirty-one artillery guns were captured by the enemy.

May 31st

By now we had been bombed and machine-gunned for eight consecutive nights. Stragglers from the previous night's action returned to the box, bloodied and very much the worse for wear.

At around 2 p.m., for about forty minutes and without a break, we were engaged in fierce aerial action with twelve enemy planes. Sergeant Major Acres, Bombardier Stocks and Gunner Aldridge were killed, while ten of our vehicles were destroyed. We brought down three Messerschmitt 109s and damaged another. One plane flew so low that it bent the wireless aerial on Captain Seton-Watson's armoured vehicle. By now, the regiment had shot down some forty-two enemy aircraft and had inflicted severe damage on about 100 others.

At this point, the German armour had got right up on us and was in full view to our south. Vehicles from both sides were burning all around; plumes of thick acrid smoke and the smell of burning flesh hung in the air. Bursting explosives, churned-up earth and fragments of metal from the heavy shelling were everywhere. It was hell-on-earth, *the Devil's Cauldron*.

June 1st

Word came through that fifty trucks had managed to get to Bir Haleim, with badly needed water supplies. We also heard that the Germans had broken through at Sidi Muftah to our west, killing Brigadier Haydon and capturing 3,000 British troops and their equipment. This also meant that they had cut the supply route into Bir Hakeim. The Germans just kept pushing forward, attacking and destroying boxes and wiping out whole regiments as they went. Our west flank was attacked, but we managed to hold them back. That night, we were ordered to fire our guns in support of an infantry attack on Aslagh. However, the flash from the guns aided the enemy in efficiently plotting our gun pits and we came under accurate counter-fire thereafter.

June 3rd

A bad dust storm slowed down the killing for a while. In the south, General Rommel sent General Kœnig, who was holding the fort at Bir Hakeim, a hand-written note:

"To the troops of Bir Hakeim. Further resistance will only lead to pointless loss of life. You will suffer the same fate as the two brigades which were at Got el Ualeg and which were exterminated the day before yesterday - we will cease fighting as soon as you show the white flag and come towards us unarmed."

General Kœnig ignored the request, and the next day the enemy attacked again, but were pushed back.

June 4th

We were bombed and machine-gunned early this morning; I can still remember the waves of German Stuka bombers blasting a route through the minefields. You could see the special fuses that stuck out in front of the bombs; they were designed to explode above the ground and detonate the mines.

June 6th

By now, our relief convoys were getting through during the night, so we now had ammunition and supplies, including our beer ration. Ammunition dumps were built in the south west corner of the box.

We lost Captain Lanyon from H Battery; he was captured when he approached what he thought was a friendly column; it wasn't. Sgt Allan, as well as Gunners Allright and Alder were killed when their gun pit received a direct hit from a Stuka.

June 7th

All day there were swarms of bombers over Tabruk, as it continued to be heavily bombed. The enemy carried out an infantry attack on our box in an attempt to clear the minefields and allow their tanks in. They were unsuccessful, and sustained heavy casualties; the *cauldron* was now well alight.

June 8th

There was a lapse in the fighting as the enemy reorganised following their rapid gains. It was fairly quiet for a few days.

June 12th

We received orders to evacuate the box by night, although the orders were then cancelled. The enemy were now almost completely around the box and very, very close. I soon realised how close they were when I saw one of our guns receive a direct hit from a German tank. It just disintegrated, along with its crew, in a cloud of dust and smoke. I remember thinking that if we were going to leave, it needed to be soon; it felt touch and go as to whether we would make it out in time.

June 13th

We spent the day preparing to evacuate. Our orders were to head north to Akroma, to help keep the escape route along the coast road to the east open.

That evening we lined up and set off through the minefield as darkness fell. It was a moonless night, and all was quiet for the first hour or so. Then, heavy gun fire broke out from the left side of the track. German tanks had heard our convoy approaching and turned their guns towards the noise and ambushed us. I was *arse-end Charlie*, which means bringing-up the rear, along with about ten or so other trucks.

The only thing to do was to stop and beat a hasty retreat back along the track. This is what we did, leaving the front end of the convoy on fire.

As soon as the shooting had stopped, we turned into the desert and veered off to the north before continuing on our way. The upshot was that we lost fifty or so men, five of our eight guns, and several vehicles. We later heard that most of the missing became prisoners of war. We eventually reached our destination, and took up new positions in a bowl near Akroma.

The 13th June was a very bad day, and became known as *Black Saturday* throughout the Eighth Army. The Knightsbridge box was now completely abandoned, leaving behind a smouldering cauldron of death.

June 14th

We held the position at Arkoma during the day, allowing the First South African forces to pull back from the Gazala line and make for Tabruk. I remember being prepared for an enemy counter-attack, but thankfully, that never took place. At around 2 p.m. there was a dust storm that brought everything to a halt. Once it passed, we received orders to move east.

I remember we had just got my gun hooked up and ready to move, when I saw seven or eight fighter-bombers heading towards us. At first, I thought they were going for vehicles some distance away, but they suddenly turned and headed straight for me! I dived under my vehicle between the back wheels, as the bombs came down. It was all over in a few minutes, and when I came out I saw that another truck, about fifty yards from mine, had taken a direct hit; it was on fire, and shells were exploding and flying in all directions.

My first thought was to get my truck as far away from the flying debris as possible, but there was one problem. There was a large hole in the petrol tank; I could even see the petrol inside and was amazed that it had not caught fire. Upon realising the seriousness of the situation, I and a few of the lads piled into the vehicle; thankfully, it started first time, and we drove around 200 yards away before stopping. I had not noticed the planes returning, but suddenly there was a terrific explosion, flying debris, and a cloud of smoke, as a bomb landed just in front of the truck. We dived out and scattered in all directions; one of the lads made a dash for a ditch rather than staying down just as another bomb landed, and made a nasty mess of him. I can't remember his name; we dug him a quick grave, emptied his pockets, wrapped him in a blanket, and laid him to rest. There was no clergyman or officer; just myself and the remaining gun crew. With no time to hang around, we commended him to God, gave him his last salute, marked his grave with a makeshift cross, and got on our way.

June 15th

We moved through the day and by the evening we were in an area near Fort Palistrino. Here, we were told to dig in at the edge of the escarpment with a Guards Brigade.

It had been a terrible ride across the desert; our average speed was 7 mph, and we came under regular attack from enemy aircraft. I was very lucky; eleven of our lads were killed and some more of our vehicles were destroyed on our journey.

The routine was simple; on seeing aircraft or hearing the alarm, you jumped out of the vehicle and ran. I would look for an area of sand, rather than rocks, and as far away from my vehicle as possible. I would then dive for cover and lie as flat as I could. I would push the sand away with my hands, bringing my legs up and forcing sand away with my feet all at the same time, to make as big a hole as I possibly could. On one occasion, a bomb dropped a few yards from me, making a hole about ten feet deep. But I didn't get a scratch. The sand was so soft that the blast from the bomb missed me completely.

The enemy were now only a few miles south of us at El Adem; there was a real danger that if they headed north to Tabruk, we would be trapped.

June 16th

The retreating South Africans finally reached Tabruk, meaning we were ordered to evacuate eastwards. We set off at 10 a.m. on-mass; at first, we proceeded along desert tracks, until we joined the coastal road to the east of Tabruk. We were expecting to engage with the enemy in the area of Gambot; thankfully, we got through just before the Germans closed the gap and encircled Tabruk.

We received orders to report to Seventh Motor Brigade at Bir El Uesian, arriving late in the evening to be welcomed by a hot cup of tea with brandy.

In the morning, the regiment split, leaving two batteries with the Seventh Motor Brigade as a rear-guard. The enemy were now just behind us, with their columns already at Gambot. I left with the main convoy and we reached El Diedar at dusk, where we dug in for the night.

The following day we stayed where we were, carrying out maintenance, while a reconnaissance patrol was also sent out. Unfortunately, it was heavily attacked from the air, at a cost of nine trucks.

One of the crew had befriended a little terrier dog which he named Spot and kept in his haversack. Spot was a great asset, as he could tell the difference between the sound of enemy aircraft and our own. If it was an enemy aircraft, he would run to the gun pit barking, and we would be ready for action even before the alert was sounded. If it was one of ours, he would wag his tail furiously.

He was equally good when it came to vehicles. There was a story going around that Spot saved the lives of 200 soldiers in the early morning, when trucks were heard coming towards our gun emplacements. There were no patrols out and the only movement expected from that direction would have been the enemy. The gun teams were in position, rounds were loaded ready to fire, and they were waiting for the trucks to come within about 100 yards before firing. Then, all the vehicles stopped. The Sergeant was just about to order "Fire!" when he noticed Spot standing in front of him with his tail wagging. Should he trust Spot and fire a warning shot, or just open fire? At that very moment, orders could be heard in

English coming from the trucks. Once they were challenged, it turned out that they were members of the First South Africans, who had not been able to get into Tabruk and were heading east with everyone else. If it had not been for Spot, the battery would have opened fire on the convoy; Spot saved the day, or so the story goes. Although dogs were not allowed because of the problems they caused, no one was going to let Spot go after he saved so many lives.

June 19th

Another move and another day of retreat was only lightened by the fact that we came across an abandoned ration dump; everyone heaped their vehicles with crates of tinned milk, bacon and fruit.

June 20th
The fall of Tabruk

At 5.20 a.m., as the first rays of sunlight began to creep over the desert, long black lines of enemy tanks, trucks and infantry slowly started to move towards Tabruk. As the noise grew louder and got closer, small black dots appeared on the horizon which, as they drew nearer, became waves of Stukas and Junker 88s. Every airworthy enemy plane in North Africa had been pressed into service for the battle that day. As heavy enemy artillery began to fire, their planes released bombs and quickly got out of the way, making room for the next wave. They pounded a gap in the defensive perimeter 600 yards wide. Then, under the cover of an artillery barrage and half-hidden by smoke and dust, German and Italian sappers raced forward to lift mines and bridge the tank traps, allowing tanks and infantry to race through the gap. As they moved forward, they lit green, red and purple flares and the Stukas dropped their bombs just ahead of the advancing, multi-coloured smoke screen.

The timing of the entire operation was perfect. The first shock troops broke into the fortress from the south east. A second group breached the defences in the south, along the El Adem road. As tanks poured into the city, they fanned out and headed for the harbour, while parachutists were dropped to disorganise the defences and protect the supply dumps from demolition.

By dawn the next day, Tabruk was a pile of ruins. The streets were a maze of rubble; in the harbour the masts and funnels of sunken ships rose pathetically from the water, and a large white flag flew over the now empty Sixth Brigade Headquarters. The signal to surrender created confusion; some units never received the message, while others, such as the 3rd Coldstream Guards, ignored it and escaped. The Cameron Highlanders, along with remnants of some of the Indian Brigades, held out for more than twenty-four hours. They only surrendered after being told by the Germans that if they did not, they would concentrate every piece of artillery in Tabruk on their position. Finally giving in, they marched down to the prisoners of war cage in parade formation, with the pipes skirling, *The March of the Cameron Men*. As they approached, every man along the way, prisoner and German sentry alike, snapped to attention.

After two years in British hands, Tabruk had fallen in just two days; the Battle of Gazala was over, and we were retreating eastwards as fast as we could go...

On June 22nd, Rommel received a message from Hitler, informing him that at the age of 49 he had just been appointed Germany's youngest Field Marshal. Rommel celebrated that night with canned pineapple and a small glass of whisky. After dinner he wrote to his wife..."Hitler has made me a Field Marshal. I would much rather he had given me one more division."

After the war, the remains of those commonwealth troops who gave their lives, were gathered from the battlefield burial grounds and from scattered desert sites and transferred to the Knightsbridge War Cemetery. There are 3,651 servicemen commemorated and 993 of the burials are unidentified. The Knightsbridge War Cemetery is located about fifteen miles west of Tabruk, near Acroma.

The German War Cemetery is located in Tabruk and contains 6,026 burials.

11

The Defence at El Alamein

June 22nd

At dusk, we left the command of the Fifth Infantry Brigade; they remained behind at Sollum with our H Battery, to form a rear-guard, whilst I and the rest of the regiment left during the night. We passed into Egypt at some stage, before arriving at Bir El Khamsa around noon the next day. We were now in full retreat; there were two signal flags being used for the convoy — a blue flag, which indicated proceed in a forward direction, and a red flag, which meant stop. There was no signal for going back.

Off we went, bumping over the desert scrub; I had a scarf wrapped around my face to protect me from the clouds of dust and sand, and I was swearing and cursing as we drove into the unknown. We were living like Bedouins and the battery had taken on the appearance of a band of Afghan tribesmen. My uniform was now just rags, I was covered in lice and desert sores, and my vehicle and I had to be coaxed along. Only those who have experienced a dreadful long desert journey know how tired and exhausted the body can become. The dust and dirt cling to your skin, your eyes become red and bloodshot, your head aches, and your limbs become stiff. After a while, I became like a zombie, doing things automatically and reacting to events without knowing why. I think my mind went blank as we drove through the night; I just followed the truck ahead and waited for the next attack.

On the 24th, we moved off from Bir El Khamsa at around 6 a.m. We proceeded along the escarpment, in an area ten miles south west of Bagush, with orders to find and report to the Twenty-second Armoured Brigade. We eventually found them the following day at Sidi Hamza. At some stage during the day, we were joined by H Battery, who had remained behind as rear-guard; it was a great relief to see them return to the fold.

We were heavily bombed during the night of the 25th by our own Wellington bombers; they caused lots of damage and a few people sustained injuries. To make things worse, we were then ordered to move back west towards the enemy, in order to engage them at first light.

There was a saying at the time;
If the Germans bombed, we would run,
If the British bombed, the Germans would run,
If the Italians bombed, everyone ran!

June 28th

The enemy turned out to be four Italian motorcyclists, followed by a staff car, a general's caravan, and a long column of tanks neatly dressed two by two. Within minutes, at least nine tanks had been destroyed and the Italians had fled. They soon counter-attacked with twenty or so tanks; H Battery supported the Queens Bays and forced them to move north.

That evening, we were given orders to move back south east towards the Alamein area. We travelled through the night deep into the desert, travelling using a compass and the stars, as there were no roads. At one point, I got stuck in a desert bog and my truck went down to its underside. Unable to reverse, we used a tank to pull her out.

Not long after this, we came to a wadi, with thirty-foot walls on either side. It was there that we came across several abandoned three-ton trucks, all belonging to the Royal Army Service Corps. This was our first proper stop since leaving the desert bog, so we decided to rest for a while and have a look around the trucks to see what we could scrounge. Then we got a surprise; one of the lads took his spade *for a walk* up onto the ridge. He looked over the top and saw an Italian gun battery with their guns pointing in the direction which we wanted to travel. We did not have the ammunition to engage in a fight, so came up with a cunning plan. We decided that a few of the lads should walk up to the ridge and let the enemy see them. This paid off, and the Italians hitched-up their guns and left via another dried-up riverbed, around a corner and out of sight. We then quickly got on our way, and were about a mile away when the Italians started shelling the position we had just left with high explosive shells. We were now playing hide and seek with the enemy, relying on our desert knowledge and skill to outwit them.

June 30th

That evening, the German Twenty-first Panzer Division passed within a thousand yards of us; we were under orders to remain quiet and to avoid detection. I didn't need to be told twice! This meant that the Germans were ahead of us and we were now behind enemy lines.

The following morning, we continued to head east, but met with the rear of the Panzer Division from the night before and engaged with some success, taking prisoners and destroying a few tanks. Later, they counter-attacked with sixteen tanks. We were still on the move with the Bays, but their tanks were running very low on petrol; if they stopped, we would be defenceless and in a very precarious position.

July 1st

We set off at first light, heading north this time for about twelve miles before turning east, with the remains of the regiment being led by tanks from the Bays. Moving across the desert is not easy; we would normally navigate using a sun compass, but I didn't have one. As there were no landmarks to head towards, I improvised by tying a piece of string from the bonnet to the top of the windscreen. This cast a shadow onto the bonnet, so all I had to do was keep the shadow in the same position, to be confident I was heading in the right direction. Whenever we stopped I would check the tyres and let some air out so they wouldn't burst in the heat. After a quick check to see if any sand had gotten into the carburettor, petrol, oil, water or my weapon, we would be on our way.

By some miracle, we made it through all of the enemy lines without detection, and that evening we arrived at our destination, fifteen miles south of the Al Alamein railway station. I was absolutely exhausted, and so were the enemy. I didn't know it at the time, but the plan was to check the enemies' advance at this point, and that is exactly what happened. We remained firm in that area, enduring some terrible attacks reminiscent of those I had experienced at Knightsbridge. This was the defence of El Alamein. Since, historians have called it by several other more glamorous names, including the first Battle of El Alamein, and the Battle of Mersa Matruh.

July 4th

On the afternoon of the 4th, we found ourselves four miles north of Dihmaniya when they attacked with what felt like 100 tanks and Stukas. We shot down four planes and knocked out about thirty tanks before they stopped their attack. Sadly, Captain Lawery and many others were killed. The following day, we moved to the west of Ruweisat and into an area known as Barrel Ridge, where we dug gun pits; it soon became clear that we were there to stay. Over the next few days, Rommel ordered his Afrikakorps to resume its attack on the Ruweisat ridge in an attempt to take the coastal road area.

At the same time as we were engaging the enemy, in Cairo there was something of a panic which became known as *the flap*, because they believed the Germans were on their way into the city. At the British headquarters and the embassy they burnt piles of classified papers, showering the city with ash and charred documents — a day which became known as *Ash Wednesday*.

July 6th

We started to receive placements, sixty at first, but not enough to bring our numbers up to full strength. This was a stark reminder of how many people we had lost over the past month. Things got a little quieter; there was the occasional exchange of artillery fire and Stuka attack, but the enemy had started to move back and dig their own main defensive positions out of range of our heavy guns.

One morning, at first light, we were in our stand-to position when one of the enemy in a forward observation post about 600 yards away climbed out of his hole and started to pee. I stood there watching, not believing my eyes, and expecting someone to shoot him at any moment. Instead, all I could hear was laughing. At that point, somebody from our side climbed out and did the same. Before you knew it, there must have been thirty people, from both sides, standing around peeing and waving at each other. This went on for about five minutes, before shells started to fall; we all dived for cover, and the war continued.

By now, the regulation army issue of two blankets had been supplemented with stuff salvaged from captured enemy vehicles. One of my prized possessions was an Italian sleeping bag; it was a bit smelly, but very comfortable. Whenever I could, I would lie down underneath or by the side of my truck. Due to the intense heat, I would use the sleeping bag as a mattress and lie there staring at the stars. I would think about how they had been there for millions of years and that we are on this tiny planet for just a few short years, but spent a great deal of that time killing each other. I would eventually fall sleep, only to be rudely awoken by the first rays of the day, the obligatory *stand-to*, and the ever-present army of flies, bullets and bombs. As well as the tradecraft of war and survival, I had also learnt the black art of scrounging and trading in rations, equipment and clothing.

July 13th

We were now well dug-in, and so were the enemy. Over the next few weeks, the enemy attacked us in different locations, trying to find a gap or weaknesses in our defence. Most of the action took place on and around the Kuwiest Ridge to our north, and involved the New Zealanders; their worst day was on the 16th, when they took heavy casualties during a German counter-attack. We were also engaged in a few small skirmishes, but they ran into our minefields and stiff defensive positions. It was fairly quiet for all the anti-aircraft crews, as the RAF was in the air carrying out heavy bombing and strafing attacks on the enemy positions.

On one occasion, I was taking things easy, writing letters, reading when in the distance I heard the sound of aeroplane engines; before I knew it, the aircraft were upon us. Our orders were not to engage, as the RAF was supposed to be flying overhead — not in this case, however! Everyone ran to the nearest trenches and dived in. They were just flying around in circles dropping their bombs, without a care. I was a little slow getting to the trench; I threw myself in only to find myself on top of two other gunners who had got there before me. All I can remember was being worried that my backside was sticking up outside the trench with shrapnel flying around everywhere, and all the bad language coming from the two men stuck below me.

Those pilots were very brave. They would nosedive their aircraft through a barrage which could destroy them and the plane at any moment, then drop their bombs, with everybody firing at them with anything they could muster. On occasions, they flew so low and so close, you could see their faces as we threw rocks at them.

It was at this point that Rommel decided his exhausted forces could make no further headway without resting and regrouping.

12

Churchill Drops in for a Brew

August 1942

I was now in a pretty poor state of health, and along with eighty others in the battery I was being treated for desert sores; around twenty other men were sick with various other ailments, such as *gippy-tum*. I had well and truly gone through *le baptéme du fer*, my baptism under fire, and my knees were brown to boot. I was familiar with battlefield noises, and was able to separate the sound of bullets which were passing me and of no danger from that of bullets which were *effective* and aimed at me; I could even tell how far away the bullets had been fired from, and which direction. I could tell with my eyes closed when a Stuka had dropped its bomb and was pulling out of its dive, or when a fighter had extended its firing zone and was no longer a threat. I knew which direction to run, for how long, and where best to hide and I could operate every position on the gun blindfolded, even by myself if needed.

Now that things had quietened down, on the 1st and 2nd, the *top-brass* showed up to carry out an inspection. General 'Tartan Tam' Wimberley visited, along with our old Commanding Officer, Brigadier Vaughan-Hughes, who had left us the previous month to take command of the Seventh Motor Brigade Group; also visiting was Brigadier Fowler, Commander of the First Armoured Brigade.

The next day we were told that the division was being sent to the rear for refit and reconstruction. Whilst I was looking forward to moving off the line, it was a sad time. I had lost many of my chums, killed or missing, and now some of us who remained were being attached, with our equipment, to 1 RHA, so it could be brought up to strength, whilst others were transferred to different units.

Looking back, splitting us up and moving us around seemed like a bad idea at the time, and especially the changes to the officers. However, I now appreciate how hard it must have been to lead men in such arduous conditions, and how absolutely worn-out they must have been. To relieve them of their commands, take them back to HQ for a short while, and give them new duties whilst they rebuilt their minds and bodies showed considerable leadership, especially when you consider how precarious the situation was. Previously Generals just left everyone in the field until they broke.

We soon moved off the Alamein line, back ten miles to a bivouac area near Deir El Tarfa. On arrival, we were greeted by the Quartermaster, who gave us new uniforms and access to a mobile bath house. I was washed, de-loused and put into a clean new uniform, given hot food made in a cookhouse, and then stood in a queue at a NAFFI wagon to buy cigarettes and pop.

Here, I briefly came under the command of 1 RHA, still part of the Twenty-second Armoured Brigade, but I was assigned as *Army Reserve* whilst we refitted. However, this also meant that we were required to be available, if called upon, to deal with any breakthrough on any section of the front. There was a rumour going around that there was going to be a German attack on the 15th August, so we didn't sit around resting for long.

A lot happened over the next few weeks that changed everything. General 'Auk' Auchinleck was at the time wearing two hats — as the Commander-in-Chief of the Middle East Command, and as the Commander of the Eighth Army. Winston Churchill was not happy with the way the war in Africa was going, and replaced him, making General Alexander the Commander of the Middle East, and General Gott Commander of the Eighth Army.

On the 6th August, we were on manoeuvres, practicing rapid deployment and building defensive positions in the *Partridge* area, which was north east of the bivouac. Thankfully, we had the assistance of bulldozers and pneumatic drills helping us to dig in our guns. It was there that I heard Gott had been killed when his plane was shot down en route to Cairo by two German Messerschmitt 109 fighters, killing everyone on board.

His replacement was a Lieutenant-General Bernard Montgomery, who took over command on the 13th August, the same day we held a memorial and thanksgiving service in the cinema for those we had lost. Montgomery's first order was that all contingency plans for retreat were to be destroyed; "I have cancelled the plan for withdrawal," he said. "If we are attacked, then there will be no retreat. If we cannot stay here alive, then we will stay here dead."

On the 15th, two significant things happened. We had a visit from General Renton, who ordered that eight men per week in each battery were to be given three days' leave, and the German infantry attacked as anticipated on the New Zealand front; it was all over by 10 a.m., and we never moved from the bivouac area. Life went on as normal, and I was waiting for my turn for leave.

Our daily ration of water in the field was about half a gallon each, and was used for everything. I never drank the water on its own if I could help it. It was often distilled seawater and too foul to drink — warm, salty, and never quenched your thirst. It was much better to have it in a mug of sweet scalding tea, or *char*. Despite the tinned milk often curdling, a *cuppa char* was always most welcome. It's true to say that the battery's morale could be measured by our supply of tea. This fact was not lost on those in charge, and I believe the British government bought tea by the ton just to keep the army supplied. Beer was in short supply in the desert, and the only other thing after *char* that could quench my thirst was lemonade, which I would buy from the NAFFI truck whenever I got the chance. I would completely fill my haversack, because you never knew when you would get the chance to resupply. My haversack would never leave my side; if it did, its contents would have been stolen faster than you could blink. Thirst is a terrible thing; it gets to the stage when it's all you can think about. I would lay awake at night thinking of babbling streams, cider, and, of course, lemonade. There were times in the desert when I swore that I would never complain about anything in life, so long as I had water. To this day, these thoughts have helped me to survive. When everything under the sun appears to be going wrong and my whole world is crashing down, I stop and ask myself a simple question: do I have water? If the answer is yes, then everything will be okay!

Necessity has always been the mother of invention, and we found different ways of conserving and using our limited water supplies. We would *pool* it for washing, tossing a coin or taking turns as to who had the privilege of washing first in the morning. The last man usually gave up his wash for the day, and myths that we hadn't had a proper wash in months were true. If we were near a water supply we would shower or bath using cut-down petrol cans with holes punched in to act as a shower sprinkler, or a tarpaulin sheet from off a truck, placed in a trench to form a makeshift bath tub. The regimental water carts usually managed to visit us at least twice a week; when they arrived, the call would go out, "Water–cart-up", and we would fall over each other to get to them, loading up Jerry cans and any other available container.

In addition to my Italian sleeping bag, I had an Italian gas mask. This was a prized possession, as the filter was excellent for recycling water. I made a primitive filtration system using an old water can as a trough, and placed the gas mask filter on a frame above it. Once I had cleaned my teeth, I would swill out my mouth and spit into the filter, where it eventually ran through and into the tin can below. This same process was followed after washing and shaving, and so on. I would then use the filtered water to wash socks, and the process was repeated. Eventually, the water would end up in the radiator of my truck. This had an added benefit, as once the radiator warmed-up, the lavender scent from the shaving foam would fill the cab.

Another desert skill was finding water; this included locating wells, which were often to our south near the Qattara Depression and close to the enemy. Sometimes you would arrive near a well to find it occupied by the enemy. If this happened, we would hold back and wait our turn, and this worked both ways; no hostility or fraternisation, just desert courtesy.

Whilst water was constantly in short supply, there always seemed to be plenty of food, but it was often unpalatable.

In the morning, as soon as I heard the stand down whistle, I would first make breakfast, which started with a cuppa char; to eat would be biscuit, or *burgoo*; this term referred to army biscuits soaked overnight in water, with tinned milk and sugar added to give flavour. The main meal of the day was often in the evening. The standard diet was bully beef fritters, or tinned meat and vegetables, with dehydrated potatoes made into a stew. This would sometimes be complemented with enemy rations that I had picked up on the way, or the occasional tablespoon of curry powder.

On the 20th, we were visited by the Prime Minister, Winston Churchill, as well as General Allen Brooks, Alexander, and Montgomery; there were lots of speeches and smiles all around. Montgomery was even handing out cigarettes, but I was too far away to grab one.

On the 24th August, there was a full moon; all leave was suspended and we were put on eight hours' notice to move, as an enemy attack was imminent. Nothing happened, and on the 26th it changed to two hours to move.

On the 28th August, we spent the night beside the Cairo to Alexander road. The next day, at 4 a.m., the Germans attacked the front line, but we were already on the move to the Alaza camp for a refit. On arrival, we were confined to camp but still on two hours' notice to move.

On the 31st, military awards were announced; there was a gallantry medal for Major Worthington, who received a Distinguished Service Order (DSO), and Military Medals (MM) for bravery were awarded to Lance Bombardier White and Gunners Knowles and Zammil; Sergeant Jones also received a bar for his MM.

There was no more serious fighting anywhere along the front over the next few months, as both sides prepared. My lasting impression of that period was the endless movement, as the division underwent continuous training. During the day, I was driven crazy by the heat, the millions of flies, and the dust-storms; at night, the bed-bugs, cockroaches and lice took over. There was the endless digging of gun-pits and slit-trenches in hard desert ground, and the nightly guard duties. However, my fondest memory was how, every evening, we would tune into Belgrade radio, to listen and sing along to 'Lili Marlene'.

13
Fare-thee-well Lili Marlene

The story behind the song *'Lili Marlene'* will sound a little farfetched, but I lived through some of the story, so I know that part of it is true. The rest I learnt about after the war, and like the *lady in white* at Durban harbour, it is a story of the time, made more real by the events we were living through.

It started life in 1915 as an anti-war poem, written by a young German soldier called Hans Leip, whilst in the World War One trenches. The poem, called *'The Song of a Young Soldier on Watch'*, was a love poem about his girlfriend Lili, a grocer's daughter from Hamburg, and Marlène, a French nurse he knew. She would wave at him and the guard sentry on her way to the field hospital every morning. The first verse reads;

> *In the dark of evening where you stand and wait,*
> *Hangs a lantern gleaming by the Barrack gate,*
> *We'll meet again by lantern shine,*
> *As we did once upon a time,*
> *We to, Lile Marlaine,*
> *We to, Lilie Marlaine.*

In 1937, Hans published a collection of poems, including this one, under the title *'Die Hafenorgel'* — *'The Little Organ by the Harbour'*. A German composer named Norbert Schultze read the poem and liked it enough to write a melody, adding two more verses; he put it to music and called it *'Das Mädchen unter der Laterne'* — *'The Girl under the Lantern'*. He convinced a popular Swedish singer working the clubs in Berlin, Lale

Andersen, to record the song just before the outbreak of the war in 1939, under the title *'Lili Marlene'*.

The song was a flop; in Germany, it was seen as an anti-war song and not of a military style preferred by the Nazi party, meaning it was banned. Both Norbert and Lale were charged with *moral sabotage of the nation's aims*. Lale was arrested, and Norbert was made to compose Nazi- approved musical pieces.

In 1941, Germany invaded Yugoslavia, occupied Belgrade, and used the city's radio station to transmit propaganda and political speeches from the renamed *Soldatensender Belgra'* — Soldiers' Radio Belgrade. From there, they were able to broadcast to their troops in Africa and the Mediterranean. Shortly after the German Propaganda Company took occupation of the radio station, local partisans bombed it, smashing most of the record collection, and leaving them desperately short of music to play in-between communiqués. One record that survived was Lili Marlene, and with precious little else to play, it was broadcast. From its first transmission, the catchy tune, with its slightly sickly sentimental words, became a *smash hit* with German troops, who requested that the song be played again. Eventually, and with Rommel's intervention, the Nazis retracted the ban.

Every evening at 9.55 p.m., following the radio programme *'Messages from home, to forces at the front'*, the station would close down for the night; but as this happened, the Bugle call introduction could be heard as the song was played. Andersen became a star, and toured singing the song. Cafe-bar shops were opened in her name, and statues erected; she was recruited to help raise funds for the Nazi war effort.

As for the Eighth Army, there were very few radios at the front. Every evening, around 9 p.m., we would make our way to the radio truck, drawn towards the light on the radio dial like moths to a flame. At first, the radio would be tuned into the nightly BBC Home Service broadcast. Once that had finished, the radio would then be tuned into the Belgrade station to hear the end of *'Messages from home'*. We would often sit in silence, with just the glow from pipes and cigarettes to indicate who was there, just waiting for that song about a sentry and a lamp post, and thoughts of home, our sweethearts, and leaving Cairo.

I have heard the song more times that I can remember, and can still hear all the different versions in my head. It makes me smile every time I hear it, and takes me straight back to the first time I heard it in 1942, just before the Battle of El Alamein, sitting peacefully with my chums, staring at the stars. The sound drifted across the great open expanse of the North African desert; her voice seemed to reach out; husky, sensuous, nostalgic and sugar-sweet, as she lingered over every word of the gentle melody.

The song became the official marching song of the Italians; it even became the unofficial song of the Eighth Army. Other versions were made; a popular one was by Marlene Dietrich, which was translated into English and sung by Anne Shelton and Vera Lynn. There was even an English propaganda version transmitted back to the Germans. It goes without saying that there were also numerous local versions, most of which were crude, such as *'Dirty Gerty From Bizerte,'*; Bizerte is a port in Tunisia, and the song was sung throughout the bars in Cairo, Alex and beyond.

Dirty Gertie from Bizerte,
Hid a mousetrap 'neath her skirtie,
Strapped it to her kneecap purty,
Baited it with Fleur de Flirte,
Made her boyfriends' fingers hurty,
Made her boyfriends most alerte!
She was voted in Bizerte,
Miss Latrine for 1930...

14

Operation Bertram

September 1942

The beginning of September brought about lots of change, as the Eighth Army reorganised itself. It was hard to keep track of what was going on, as things changed so fast. On the 1st, I was back with the Second Royal Horse Artillery under the command of Headquarters Battery. At first, I was told that the regiment was going to become part of the Nile Valley force, operating in the Khatatba area. The following day our orders changed and we were to operate in the Middle East, North Africa, also known as the MENA area, under the command of the Fifty-first Division. By the 4th September, we were under the command of the Tenth Independent Motor Brigade, and on the 5th the regiment lost its anti-tank capability and was sent to join the 102nd Anti-Tank Regiment. Three days later, I was back under the command of headquarters, and on twenty-four hours' notice to move.

On the 16th September, we had a change of Commanding Officer; we lost Colonel Bolton, who took over command of an Indian Armoured Division, and Colonel Cowan assumed command of the regiment. Cowan was a grammar school boy type; he mumbled all the time, with "urms", "ars" and "yars". We had little confidence in him, and when he was out of earshot, we would say, "We're all going to die." I recall he collected cigarette cards, which he traded for treats. His general philosophy was to keep us busy at all times. This meant keeping us away from *dirty things*, like the out of bounds areas.

Over the following weeks, we embarked on night and day training exercises. We practiced moving to our assembly area by passing in a single file through minefields, from where we deployed in darkness to our firing positions; this was made difficult by the introduction of obstacles and mines by the training instructors. Once in position, we would wait for first light and then practice target locating, followed by barrages of various types of concentration, before returning to the bivouac to rest and prepare for the next exercise.

The weather suddenly changed as the desert's winter season arrived; it was cooler during the day and freezing at night.

There was no more sleeping out under the stars, and a more practical solution was created, with the help of a bulldozer and two ten-man 'tipi' tents. First, we dug a pit fifteen feet square and ten feet deep. Then we turned one of the tents upside down to cover the floor and the walls of the hole. The other tent was then spread over the top and boulders spread all the way around the edge to keep it in position and to stop it blowing away. It was very comfortable inside, especially when a sandstorm was raging outside.

There was little you could do when a sandstorm struck; I would get a wet scarf or rag to wrap around my face and mouth, put on my goggles and, if in the open, find a large rock to crouch behind until it passed over. I would then spend the rest of the day shaking the sand out of my hair, boots and clothing, as it got everywhere. This was also the season of rain storms, which caused flash floods; these floods would very quickly fill the wadis, which only a few weeks earlier had been a safe haven, with a wall of moving water, twenty feet high, washing away equipment and drowning anyone unlucky enough to be in its way.

September drifted into October and the promised three days' leave never came. I knew that something 'big' was going to happen soon; training intensified and supplies were being built up.

The front line covered a relatively short distance of about thirty miles. It stretched from the Mediterranean Sea in the north, near El Alamein railway station, down to the impassable Qattara Depression in the south. There was a constant movement of troops and equipment up and down the line; most like me were engaged in training and familiarisation. I got to know the whole area like the back of my hand; every track, wadi, fire position, escarpment silhouette, and the location of the *real* supply dumps.

What was going on at the time was an elaborate top-secret deception, designed to make Rommel believe that any attack would happen in the south. Far away from the coast road and railway where it eventually happened, and a lot sooner than his intelligence had expected. The deception was codenamed *Operation Bertram,* and involved physical deceptions, using dummy vehicles and clever camouflage. There was also another operation, called *Canwell,* which took place at the same time and involved false radio traffic, which complemented the ruse.

Bertram created the appearance of a ghost army in the south and involved hiding troops, equipment and supplies in the north. Dummy artillery guns were made from local materials to fool the enemy, and our real guns were disguised as trucks, using quick-erect canopies called *sunshields*. These shields were built by three companies of pioneers from the secretive A Force, also known as the *Magic Gang*. They were masters of illusion and confusion on a grand scale, using methods developed from stage magicians to make objects disappear or appear as something else. The magic brain was Jasper Maskelyne, or to use his stage name, *Maskelyne the Magnificent*, the master of make-believe; at the time, he was working for Military Intelligence, Section Nine (MI9) in Cairo, but was drafted-in to help with the operation.

How it worked was very clever. In the bivouac area, we parked real supply trucks out in the open; these were seen by the enemy as *soft targets*, of no real value, and not worth attacking.

At the same time, real artillery guns would be left in-plain view in supply areas close to the ports, some considerable distance away from the front line, where they would be needed if an attack were to take place. The aim was for enemy reconnaissance planes and spies to spot the guns and become familiar with their locations. Then, during the night and in secret, the real guns were moved into the bivouac and occupied the same positions as the supply trucks and were covered with *sunshields*. Then dummy guns replaced the ones we moved, giving Rommel the impression that our guns were still several days journey behind the front line. We also stacked our water and petrol cans along the sides of trenches so they were hidden in the shadows. Our rations were stacked into a shape, which when draped with camouflage netting gave the appearance of trucks. There was even a dummy water pipeline constructed in the south, at an apparent rate of five miles per day, again indicating we would not be ready to attack for weeks.

Montgomery came and inspected us on the 3rd October, and a few days later the division moved west into the desert, two miles south of Gebel El Tibabi, to another bivouac area. From there I was sent to El Imayid railway station, where hundreds of *sunshield* trucks were pre-positioned in neat lines and numbered. My Matador tractor and anti-aircraft gun had a very distinctive shape. The pioneers had made shields to fit over them, which magically transformed them into British three-ton trucks. I was allocated two numbers — one for the tractor, and one for the gun — and was taken to where they were located. I was then taught how to take the *sunshield* down, store it for transportation, and then how to put them up again — a skill which I had to perfect at night! Once the pioneers were satisfied that I knew what to do, I returned to the bivouac with my secret cargo of *sunshields*.

As well as hiding our preparations in the north, which involved making hundreds of tanks, field guns and thousands of tons of supplies disappear, dummy tanks, guns and supplies were constructed in the south, giving the impression that an Armoured Corps of 600 vehicles was concentrating in the area.

In the south, we used the same principle in reverse. We dug gun pits and laid our guns in the Murrayfield and Meltingpot zones. Then, during the night we moved out, and dummy replacements were put in place. When we returned to the bivouac site the guns were camouflaged using *sunshields*.

For the first few weeks in October the RAF had established air superiority along the front, which meant enemy aircraft reconnaissance operations were limited, which aided the deception. This also meant that there was little anti-aircraft action for me, so I spent most of my time on spotter duty.

Things changed pace on the 15th and 16th, when we carried out dress rehearsal exercises involving passing through minefields and deploying into no man's land in support of advancing troops. We were also ordered to drive our trucks around one of the dummy supply dumps; it had a proper filling station and life-size dummy soldiers made of straw. On the 16th, a violent sandstorm hit the area, complete with driving rain, that blew most of the night, destroying many of the dummy vehicles. The pioneers worked through the night to make do and mend, and by the morning the sandstorm had passed and everything was as it had been before.

On the 19th October, just after first light, we packed our equipment and left the bivouac. This time it was not an exercise, and everyone knew that the battle would soon start. The whole division was on the move; this included around fifty trucks which were going to be used on the deception. We travelled through the day and into the night, eventually covering sixty miles, mostly along the Alexander Road to the staging area near Shaltut, twelve miles west of a staging area known as Kilo 152; we arrived at 1.30 a.m. the next day. The area had previously been occupied for some considerable time by New Zealanders, so it was a simple case of taking over their old dugouts and laying the guns.

There was no time to rest; the order was for full camouflage of the heavy equipment and there was to be no more movement. The anti-aircraft guns were to operate as normal, just as if the New Zealanders were still in residence. The trucks were poorly camouflaged so they could be seen by the enemy. All this preparation meant it was several hours before I was able to close my eyes.

Barely an hour passed before I was woken for stand-to. Shortly after the whistle went off to stand down, I sat to have my breakfast cuppa *char* and *burgoo*, but at that point the call for action came. This was despite the RAF being overhead; they were worried that the hoax would be discovered, so it was a calculated risk to allow us to fire. We opened up on enemy fighters that were flying around looking for targets of opportunity. We brought down two aircraft; only one of the pilots parachuted clear of his burning craft, and was taken prisoner.

On the 21st, at last light, we engaged more enemy aircraft, and once it was sufficiently dark the switch took place. I drove a truck back to the supply area and collected a matador and anti-aircraft gun, before returning to the bivouac where I covered it with the shields.

The following day, orders were received that tomorrow would be day one of *'Operation Lightfoot'*, and on the afternoon of the 23rd October, final orders for the attack came and the Battle of El Alamein began.

There was a saying, "He who dives last, dies first."

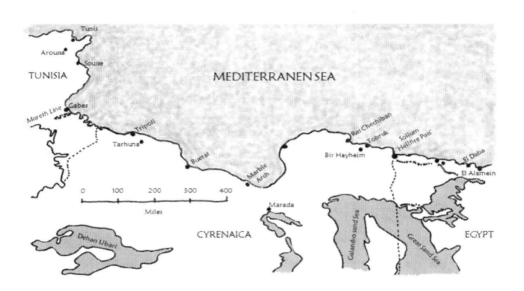

15

The Battle of El Alamein
2rd October to 4th November 1942

The Battle of El Alamein consisted of three stages: the Break-in, the Dog Fight, and the Break-out. The plan involved a prolonged and accurate bombardment at the beginning of the battle to destroy the power of the enemy before attacking with infantry, followed by tanks; this was the *Break-in* stage. After that, there would be a period of aggressive engagements, the *Dog Fight*, with the aim of punching our way through the enemy defences and twenty miles of minefields. Once through all that, it would be time for the *Break-out* stage. This would be the forced retreat of the enemy, with me and the rest of the Eighth Army in hot pursuit.

My job was to provide anti-aircraft cover for the Headquarters of Second Field Regiment, Royal Horse Artillery. The Royal Horse Artillery, in turn, provided artillery support to the First Armoured Division under the command of Major General Briggs. Whilst I didn't know it at the time, I was to meet Major General Briggs at the end of the battle, in what would turn out to be a costly encounter.

Prior to the battle, on the evening of the 23rd, a message from General Montgomery was read to all troops.

"When I assumed command of the Eighth Army, I said that the mandate was to destroy Rommel and his army and that it would be done as soon as we were ready. We are ready now.

The battle which is now about to begin will be one of the decisive battles of history. It will be the turning point of the war: The eyes of the whole world will be on us, watching anxiously which way the battle will swing. We can give them their answer at once: "It will swing our way."

We have first-class equipment; good tanks, good anti-tank guns; plenty of artillery; and plenty of ammunition; and we are backed up by the finest air-striking force in the world.

All that is necessary is that each one of us, every officer and man, should enter this battle with the determination to see it through---to fight and to kill---and finally to win. If we all do this there can be only one result---together we will hit the enemy for six, right out of North Africa. Let us all pray that the Lord mighty in battle will give us the victory.

There was also another message, which is not often reported; *"Everyone must be imbued with the desire to kill Germans, even the padres – one for weekdays and two on Sundays."*

The Break-in, 23rd October

On so many occasions previously, I had written and re-written my last letters home, just in case. Because of this, the waiting for a battle to start was always the worst part, so I was glad when, to the west of our position, at 9.40 p.m., the barrage began. Even though I knew it was coming, I distinctly remember being surprised by the terrible and continuous force of the 1,200 guns; the blinding flashes, the smell of cordite, and the deafening noise — so loud it almost burst my eardrums. The flashes lit up the sky, and in the distance I could see the continuous explosions of the shells hitting their targets. The colossal bombardment continued along the entire front until 10 p.m., after which it became more sporadic and less intense. When the lull in the firing came, it was quiet enough that I could hear the wail of the Scottish bagpipes, as the 5,000 men of the Fifty-first Highland Infantry moved forward, with orders not to stop for the dead or wounded. Even from a distance, the music made the hairs on the back of my neck stand up. After such an accurate bombardment, the enemy must have been demoralised to hear such a sound coming towards them.

Shortly afterwards, the armour started moving forward; it was a very impressive sight, with 160 tanks and the accompanying circus on the move. We watched and waved them on their way, and soon it was our turn. At 11.40 p.m., the whole of the Second RHA set off; I left with the Headquarters section along with the reconnaissance parties and L Battery. We moved off in silence and under bright moonlight, passing through British minefields and driving westward on a dusty track designated as the 'Star route'. The route wasn't as clear of mines as promised, and we lost one truck and a tank, which were blown up by stray mines; thankfully there were no casualties.

By the morning we had entered the first of the enemy's two 40-mile-long minefields, which Rommel called the *Devil's Garden*. Added to this, the regiment was engaging the German Twenty-first Panzer Division in the area known as *Sausage Ridge* in support of the *Jocks*, who were meeting strong resistance from German and Italian forces.

There wasn't much for the Ack-Ack crews to do, as the sky was full of RAF bombers and fighters, all travelling west at the rate of one sortie every half hour.

The Dog Fight

The next morning at first light, during stand to, we got buzzed by Stukas; we let them know we were around, and put up enough flack to keep them away from our positions; no bombs were dropped. However, we were being targeted by enemy artillery, and one of the ammunition trucks received a direct hit, killing the driver and injuring others who were stood nearby. This was the first of many similar incidents over the next few weeks. Although we suffered more casualties than that first engagement, with a number of our comrades dead, we became quite used to the almost nightly raids on our positions, and it was less frightening as time went by.

The Jocks maintained their attack on Sausage Ridge, and the regiment continued supporting the assault. We were heavily shelled again during the day, and in the evening we were subjected to a counter-attack by infantry with tank support. Thankfully, they were repelled, but it was very frightening; being surrounded by minefields means there is nowhere to run or hide. The tank mines were not as scary to me as the anti-personnel mines. You could walk on a tank mine and nothing would happen, but the anti-personnel mines detonated at waist height and sent small ball-bearings out in all directions for up to 50 feet — very messy!

The next day we made slow progress moving forward, mainly because of the volume of vehicles all trying to get through small gaps in the minefields and the enemy resistance. As usual, there was a lot of confusion at times, but somehow it all seemed much better controlled than it had been in the past, and there was definitely an air of confidence.

We made our way past over-run enemy trenches, the ground churned up from where the barrage had fallen. I was glad we had not been on the receiving end; burnt-out tanks were all around, with destroyed guns and dead bodies now swollen to twice their normal size. It was a grotesque sight. This meant more flies, which seemed to have increased by millions, and the smell of death hung heavily in the air.

I remember that everyone seemed to have a black patch on their backs; it was the flies feeding off our sweat!

We came across one or two of those feared 88s, so well dug in that only the barrels appeared above ground level; no wonder they were so difficult to knock out. The 88s were initially built as anti-aircraft flack guns. The German Africa Corp discovered that they could lower the gun barrel and engage ground targets such as tanks. They had a very accurate weapon, capable of a rapid rate of fire, that proved extremely deadly against our tanks.

My personal kit increased to include a pair of binoculars recovered from a Jerry staff car, which I later traded for an Italian revolver. I also managed to get hold of some enemy petrol cans, or as we called them, *Jerricans*. They were made of heavy gauge steel and could withstand some really hard knocks. Ours were called *flimsies*; if you sneezed, they sprang a leak. This meant that the floors of our trucks were forever soaked in petrol — a sobering thought given all the fireworks going off.

The featureless terrain made map reading difficult, which didn't help with easy troop movement. There were also constant complaints coming through that our guns had been *falling-short* and hitting friendly positions; I don't think they could tell the difference between ours and theirs, but I'm sure ours were always on target.

On the evening of the 26th, we had four visits from Stukas and 109 fighters; even though we put up an intense barrage, some still got through and bombed H Battery, causing several casualties.

On the 27th we found ourselves in the area known as *Snipe,* being attacked again. It took the loss of fifty tanks to halt the enemy advance this time.

Just after 4 p.m. we moved three miles west along route *Moon,* and halted at the edge of an enemy minefield. The designated area was already full of other units, which meant there was little space available, so some of the regiment remained behind. Minefields were proving to be the big problem, as they were on a scale we had never seen before and new ones always seemed to be found where we least expected. We had a very uncomfortable night being sporadically shelled, with a direct hit on the HQ complex where I was. We also had some casualties caused by troops straying into the minefield.

The next morning we were visited by Stukas, which targeted the troops clearing gaps in the minefield, and reports came in that the enemy were concentrating to our front, with up to 86 tanks. We were braced for an enemy attack, but received orders to hold Ack-Ack fire as the RAF would be arriving. When they did arrive, it was with Baltimores, which came in for low-level attacks; they were very accurate, but many were shot down. There were also scores of enemy fighters in the air, but all we could do was watch.

After dark we moved again, ending up behind the Quattara road, where we halted. The next day we were visited by Stukas, and this time we shot two down.

The 30th October was another hellish day, with heavier than usual shelling and more Stuka attacks. We shot two down, but the day was more memorable because of the fact that we sustained three casualties when South African troops, who were firing at enemy aircraft, ended up shooting at us. I was digging my trench, with a chum of mine a few yards away doing the same, when there was a crack, followed by a sizzling wiz-whine; a tracer shell passed right between us, and exploded twenty yards away. We looked at each other, swore, and then dug faster. It was miraculous that so few of us were wounded considering the amount of ammunition that was flying around. Most of our fatalities and injuries during the battle came from enemy artillery or mines.

By the next day, reports were coming in that the Australian Ninth Division had reached the sea and cut-off a considerable number of German forces.

On the 1st November, at around 8 a.m., Stukas were sighted, but we were ordered not to engage. Not long after, they were intercepted by our fighters and we watched and cheered as several enemy aircraft were shot down in flames. There were also reports that some of the Stukas had jettisoned their bombs and they had landed on their own troops; things felt like they were looking up. The Stukas stayed away for most of the day, but re-visited in the early evening, causing minor damage.

The next day was spent preparing for Operation Supercharge, the final assault of the battle. It involved a combined attack with the New Zealanders, and two Jock Brigades supported by the Second and Eighth Armoured, as well as the seventh Motor Brigades. We moved forward to a box just west of the Raham track, next to another enemy minefield.

At 1 a.m. on the 2nd November, concentrated firing began, which continued until 4 a.m., with each gun firing over 300 high explosive rounds. At 5 a.m. the enemy returned fire, but by first light the New Zealanders had taken their objective of Tell el Aqqaqir. We continued pushing forward under intense enemy fire until around midday, when we were unable to move any further forward. The congestion was terrible; guns and troops all crammed into such a small area, making ourselves a very juicy target for the enemy.

We seemed to be there for a lifetime. We hadn't had time to dig any slit trenches, so all we could do was lay down in whatever depression we could find, as far away from our vehicles as possible, and wait until a gap in the minefield was made. It was terrifying; there was the continuous shrill of incoming shells, tearing holes in the ground, filling the air with shrapnel as they dropped amongst us. There were dead and wounded men everywhere; headless and limbless bodies, and men screaming. It's horrible to hear yells and screams coming from those around you when there is little that you can do other than to comfort each other, bandage a wound, or say "You're okay pal."

By early evening we were on the move again, along a confusing maze of tracks; it was extremely dark, and it was difficult to see anything, especially signs to show the route through the minefields. At one stage I was carefully driving the truck, following one of the crew who had a lit cigarette and was cupping it in his hands behind his back. We eventually reached our destination, having lost a couple of trucks to mines.

We didn't know it at the time, but the following day Rommel started to move his troops back, leaving rear-guard forces to delay our advance. Stuka activity was light, and they were intercepted by our fighters; the RAF seemed to have complete mastery of the skies during daylight. There were waves of Boston bombers flying overhead, in greater numbers than I had seen before, and the only bombs that were dropped on us came mainly from marauding enemy night bombers.

The following day we continued our march forward; there was much less opposition, and reports were coming in from the RAF that the enemy was withdrawing in a hurry, heading west. Unfortunately for us, we had two Stuka raids — one as usual at 9 a.m., but another at 2 p.m. when they targeted our Ack-Ack guns; a direct hit on one gun emplacement destroyed the gun and all its crew. We shot down a few planes, but it was a sad loss. If that was not bad enough, a short while later we moved to an area called Sandy Valley, just north east of Sausage Ridge. We walked straight into an enemy position and received the worst shelling so far from airbursts and bouncing high explosive shells. Our tanks were having a rough time trying to clear the enemy positions, and their losses at the hands of 88s were very heavy.

All we could do was try and get as low as possible and wait for the enemy to be killed and the minefield cleared so we could move forward. Mortar bombs dropped all around us. I couldn't see my mates for black dust, and I remember feeling very alone and scared. Finally, word came that a gap had been made and we were to move forward. This time we came under fire from *small stuff*, which means rounds from machine-guns that whistle and whine through the air. The German guns always sounded more vicious than ours, and fired more rapidly than the Bren gun; the sound would rip through the air. We eventually moved slowly through the gap, with dead bodies lying everywhere.

The next day was the 4th, and we were given orders to move forward to Alam Abu Busat, and the whole of the army moved forward. There were so many troops on the move it was difficult to tell friendly from enemy columns, and by early afternoon we were clear of the minefields and in open desert once again. At our first halt, instead of the usual *cuppa char*, we opened a case of Pilsner beer that we had liberated earlier.

The Battle of El Alamein was over, and the Break-out stage had begun. Hitler had ordered the Afrika Korps to fight to the last, but Rommel refused to carry out this order and that morning he started his retreat. 25,000 Germans and Italians had been killed or wounded in the battle — a third of his Army. We had lost 13,000 troops.

Winston Churchill said of the battle that it was the turning of the *Hinge of Fate* — the pivotal point at which the fortunes of war finally went against the Axis powers. "Before Alamein we never had a victory. After Alamein we never had a defeat" he said. He ordered church bells to ring in celebration throughout Britain and I had a really lovely *cuppa char*!

> *I love a game, I love a fight*
> *I hate the dark, I love the light*
> *I love my drink, I love my bint*
> *I am no coward, I love life*
> *'HELL' ALAMEIN*

"I was twenty-two years old at the time I fought at El Alamein. For six months all I had known was despair, death and fear from the horrors of bombardments, curtain-fire, mines, tanks, machine-guns, hand-grenades, booby-traps and Stukas. I was not alone. Everyone felt the same. All we wanted was a break, to get away from war to peace, to be human instead of living the life of hell. Often at night we would gaze up at the stars and talk of life that used to be and to when we would return to dear old Blighty Sweet dreams, even though it all

seemed so far away at times. So much had happened to us in such a short space of time, which felt like an age."

16
The Break-out

At 9 a.m. on the 5th November, we were on the move again and there was little opposition, as the enemy rear-guard had already withdrawn. We passed through Daba unopposed, and by early afternoon we had reached the railway seven miles west of the village, where we refuelled. We set off again at dusk across very rough terrain which was strewn with pits and trenches. With no moon and only the occasional flare dropped by the RAF along the coastal road to help, many vehicles were damaged en route. After about fifteen miles, we came to a halt as the troops ahead of us ran into the enemy. Not long afterwards, we were ordered to head west at speed to support the Seventh Motor Brigade, who were engaging with enemy forces. It was a mad rush, and in the confusion and darkness many vehicles were separated from the main convoy; this included myself and a few other trucks. It was at this time that an incident occurred which would become legendary within the regiment.

The enemy forces had withdrawn with such speed that they had not just abandoned troops, but also much of their equipment. So, we spent some time, whilst trying to re-locate our unit, in the honourable occupation of scrounging, in its broadest definition, or appropriation of anything not screwed down. There was so much to collect, from complete uniforms and varieties of folding furniture, to binoculars, cameras, watches and weapons. By the time we got back to the unit, there was hardly any room left in the truck and the springs were groaning under the weight of our haul.

It was at this point that we ran into General Briggs, who was stood roadside, waving down vehicles and chatting to the drivers. Later, my defence was that I was in a rush to re-join the regiment and didn't realise the difference between the cap worn by a General, which has a red band around it, and the cap worn by Military Policemen, which has a red cover. After all, I hadn't met many Generals, had I?

I had no intention of stopping for anyone, General or policeman, especially with a truck full of loot, and so with the general waving and shouting at us to stop, I drove straight past shouting; "See here, my good man, you stick to directing traffic and I will stick to driving this truck, and we'll get the war won."

The 6th November arrived, and with it heavy rain; the desert ground quickly became a quagmire. Movement was difficult, almost impossible, and the traffic on the road was now bumper-to-bumper. We also had to stay on the road through fear of getting bogged down or straying into a minefield or roadside booby-traps, which were abundant. It was an amazing sight — vehicles as far as the eyes could see. Thankfully, the Luftwaffe never made an appearance throughout the day, and despite the difficulties, we made good progress, covering thirty miles to reach Deir Khalda.

Continuing the chase became difficult; we were short of ammunition and almost out of petrol. So desperate was the situation that we didn't have enough fuel and ammo to deploy even if we had been ordered to fight. Because of this, and the weather, we took up defensive positions to wait for resupply or an enemy counter-attack, which we expected to come from the north.

Whilst some units did manage to keep in contact with the enemy, for the most part the whole Army was bogged down, which gave Rommel enough time to organise his retreat along the coast road pretty much unmolested; in the words of Brigadier Wallace, "Rain interfered with play."

The following day, the rain stopped and the ground slowly dried, but the Army Service Corps was still bogged down thirty miles to the east with our supplies, so we stayed where we were.

The incident involving General Briggs a few days earlier had come to the attention of the Commanding Officer, who was ordered to take 'immediate' action. He did, and I lost ten days' pay, but *drank-out* on the story for many years afterwards.

The next day we put all our clocks back by one hour to conform to Egyptian winter-time; this should have happened on the 1st, but was delayed as to not cause confusion during the battle. Later in the afternoon, the petrol convoy finally arrived. The ground was now firmer and we had new orders — to destroy all remaining enemy elements and to operate as if we were in an *all-round attack*.

News started to come through that the Americans had landed somewhere in north west Africa. The news was just too good to be true! There was great rejoicing and we were anxious to press on and get to Tripoli ahead of the Yanks. The 8th November 1942 was a very significant day, because now that the Americans had joined the campaign, it had become a world war — World War Two.

It now became a rapid pursuit. We first moved twenty-five miles north west, where we spent the night beside the Siwa track at the top of an escapement. On the 10th, at first light, we joined a convoy on the coastal road, which had been allocated the code word *Charing Cross*, and headed west to a junction designated as Kilo 44. The road was littered with abandoned and burnt-out vehicles, tanks, guns and equipment of all kinds, strewn out for mile after mile.

On the 11th, we finally stopped for 'maintenance and reorganisation'. This also included 'bathing parties' to the sea; the bright blue of the Mediterranean was such a tonic to our eyes after weeks of drab desert. Swimming was a great pleasure, as it brought the chance of relieving ourselves of all the accumulated desert dust. Although it was cold at night, it remained quite warm during the day until well into late November.

When it was our turn to go, we quickly made our way the two miles to the sea and despite the beach being packed with other units, we eventually found a nice grassy spot with palm trees and settled down for the day.

What we hadn't bargained for was the fact that, because of the speed of our advance, not everywhere had been searched for enemy troops. We hadn't been there long when suddenly three unarmed Germans appeared, one waving a handkerchief. Now, we were not interested in taking prisoners and ruining our first day off since anyone could remember by taking them in. One of them spoke very good English and told us how they had got left behind during the retreat several days earlier and that they were very hungry and thirsty. That settled it; we took out our special macaroni tins that we had been saving for a treat and cooked lunch. The whole thing was a very pleasant but surreal affair. Later in the day we headed back and handed them into the Military Police.

Soon the roads were full of *Jerrys* and *Ities* surrendering in their hundreds. It was a strange and sorry sight; they looked just like us, but in a different uniform. The Germans were a tough lot, with grizzly little beards and worn out clothes. There were no armed guards escorting them; instead they moved on their own, stopping to rest, sleep and eat when they wanted. Occasionally, Military Police would arrive and direct them on their way and off they went. Eventually, captured trucks were used to transport them, going backwards and forwards all day and night, ferrying prisoners; it was an incredible sight.

The next day I got my first sight of an American. We were joined by a Colonel Reynolds from the US Observer Corp on a five-day attachment. We set off early, but when we arrived at Sollum there was a tremendous traffic jam of vehicles waiting to get through Halfaya, Hellfire Pass. Either Rommel's engineers or our own air force had blasted the road that led over Sollum hill, rendering it temporarily impassable, so we 'hung around' for the rest of the day. Once the road had been repaired, we were on the move again. In places, the road was very narrow, dug into the side of the mountain, with a sheer drop on one side and a solid wall of rock on the other, with no way of jumping clear if anything happened. We waved and hurled abuse at the light anti-aircraft crews from the 150th Battery, which had been placed at intervals up the hill to protect the division. Luckily, we were not attacked by aircraft throughout the day, and by the evening of the 14th we were in Libya and back on familiar ground again.

Soon after we arrived, H Battery left us and headed off into the desert travelling via Bir Hagheim and then heading north towards Tabruk. We continued to head west in torrential rain, stopping about eight miles before Sidi Rezegh where, on the 19th November, we received the orders we had been longing for. We were to be pulled off the front line and make our way to Ras Chechiban for three weeks of maintenance, reorganisation and training. Three weeks would eventually run into three months.

We soon set up camp, dug our defensive positions, and waited for further orders. There was still a petrol shortage, so we hardly moved anywhere throughout the period, but we were on twelve hours' notice to move in the event of any enemy thrust from the west.

We spent the days on spotter duty, training, and trying to keep dry and out of the mud, which clung to your boots like dustbin lids. Once a week the bath house would arrive; this was a great treat, as the first visit to it was our first real bath since early in October. We were also joined by around twenty replacement gunners to take the place of those we had lost in the battle.

The silence was shattered just before Christmas, when intelligence was received via Sunussi tribesmen that 1,500

Germans and Italians were hiding in wadis near Cyrene. The division was ready to move and engage forthwith, but the next day the reports were found to be false, and we were stood down.

On Christmas Eve, we received orders that we would be moving out on or about the 7th January, so we made the best of times over the festive period. Christmas Day started with a carol service, followed by a large Christmas dinner served by the colonel; fresh pork, fresh chicken, tomato soup, oven-browned potatoes and cabbage. It was a very merry and delightful Christmas; no fighting, no work, plenty of good food and drink, and no relatives popping in to make it awkward!

A number of white boxes appeared, which turned out to be gifts; they contained nuts, fruit cake, Benson & Hedges cigarettes, and sweets. We were also given some Player's cigarettes donated by the Red Cross, and to wash it all down we made a punch from our issue of rum, some gin, and Italian wine we had scrounged.

It was a very peaceful time, despite the war still raging around us; as the weeks passed, the war moved further and further away to the west. I started to appreciate the lovely countryside, green grass and little white and yellow flowers everywhere. At night, we would sit wrapped up to keep out the cold and watch the sun setting in the clear sky. Once it got dark, the evening firework show would start. Tracers would shoot off at a thousand different angles, crisscrossing all over the sky, and the glowing lights of different coloured flares and rockets would dance around in the sky.

The 7th January soon came, and we discovered that we were to join an emergency supply column of 150 trucks to take supplies from the port at Tabruk to our troops in Benghasi and Agedabia. There had been terrible storms during the first week of the New Year; we had been hit by the worst sandstorms I could remember, and other storms had wrecked many ships in the port and made the harbour unusable. Supplies were urgently needed for the forward troops, and the only way to get them there was over land.

We were keen to be on our way; we knew that the Germans were partial to bombing the ports, and the sooner we were back in the desert the better. We made good time, and dropped off the supplies, but it was on the return leg that I had problems. My truck's engine had succumbed to *desert weariness*, and I found myself at the rear of the convoy being towed by another truck when we were forced off the road by a tank transporter. We had only travelled a few yards along the sandy verge, when there was a terrific 'boom', as the truck in front drove over a mine. The truck went up in flames. Luckily, the driver managed to get out, and was only slightly singed. We eventually abandoned both vehicles and hitched a lift back on another truck, returning safely to camp without any further incidents.

During the month, despite the heavy rain, training continued. There was still no movement, as fuel was in short supply, meaning that training courses were carried out in camp. As well as all the normal artillery skills, I also learnt how to lift mines and undertake booby-trap clearance. I also received a one-week pass to Derna, the Eighth Army's leave camp, which was situated by the sea between and Tabruk.

The camp had been a pre-war holiday camp for Italians and consisted of white-washed bungalows built right on the sea front. You can only imagine how much of a treat it was to live in a proper building. There was plenty to do; one evening there was a concert party in the canteen, and another evening I went to the mobile cinema where I watched the new Abbott & Costello film, 'Ride 'Em Cowboy'; it was hilarious, and featured lots of very pretty and long-legged actresses, always a welcome sight.

We walked outside the camp, where local children sold us dates and very bitter oranges at outrageous prices. This occurred because we were in Libya, where the local currency was piastres. We had been paid in British Military Authority banknotes, the lowest denomination being a one-shilling note. The locals quickly caught on to this fact, and the most insignificant purchase would cost 'a shilling'. I bought lightweight gifts to send home, such as silk scarves and handkerchiefs.

We didn't always use money; often we bartered, trading tea for fresh eggs. We once dried out some used tea, re-packaged it, and used it to trade. It worked the first time, but the next *honest* trade we made resulted in us being given bad eggs!

The much-enjoyed leave was soon over, and we travelled the sixty miles back to camp, and its discomfort, in almost complete silence.

Back at camp, the navy, army, air force, institute, NAAFI and canteens on the whole were always well stocked, and we were kept fully occupied; boxing, football and hockey matches were played against neighbouring units, and a regimental athletics meeting was held. I had a go at boxing and earnt a black eye. There were lectures, indoor games, concerts, the mobile cinema, and debates, all designed to help fill the long evenings. It was great to be able to sit down for a while with the knowledge that my time was my own. We worked on our equipment during the day and come the night we had some fairly riotous parties with radios blaring out from the canteen tent and singing coming from all directions. At times we would dwell on who had been killed or wounded, and the terrible waste which war demands.

Everybody's health was generally good, although every morning we had sick parade where most men presented themselves to the medics to be treated for desert sores or boils. The main *cure-all* treatment was a sprinkle of sulphanilamide power, which stung like hell.

On the 23rd January, we heard that Tripoli had been captured and we were impatient to re-join the fight again.

When, after the war is over, a man is asked what he did, it will be enough for him to say: "I marched with the Eighth Army."

WINSTON CHURCHILL, Tripoli, 4th February 1943

Sandy Lane, Greatgate, Staffordshire c. 1939

Bill Rushton (on the right) and me in 1942. Bill joined the 8th King's Royal Irish Hussars and we were to fight together in Libya at the Battle of Gazala, Egypt at El Alemain, and in Stoke-on-Trent pubs!

Basic Training, 207 Anti-aircraft Training Regiment RA, December 1940. I'm in the back row, fifth in from the right.

Ack-Ack Training, Sgt Street's Section, A battery. I'm in the back row, fifth in from the right, wearing the cap.

From Left to Right, Predictor, height Finder and 3.7 AAC Gun

German A-type luftmine.

The Heinkel He111H-8 Code G1+MT incident, May 1941

Sydney (on the right) and me during shore leave in Durban 1942

On the lookout for the enemy

Receiving our orders prior to the Battle of El Alamien

17
The Battle of the Mareth Line

In early February, 1943, I was sent to the artillery practice camp, Twentieth Heavy Anti-Aircraft Battery, for ten days training. On the 28th February, I returned to the regiment; it was great to be back amongst familiar faces; colleagues who I hadn't seen for weeks, and even months, had all returned from their different assignments.

"Eat, read, sleep, talk a bit, laugh a bit, worry about a rumour and hope for good bowel movements was the order of the day. The latter being the most important!"

When the time came for us to re-join the fight, we all felt that the war in Africa would soon be at an end. Back in November, the British and Americans had invaded Algeria, and *Operation Torch* had been steadily pushing the enemy into Tunisia. The Germans and Italians were now caught between the First Army on their western flank, and the eighth Army, us, on their eastern flank, in a pincer movement. They had nowhere to go, and could either stay and fight, or retreat into Italy.

After three months in the rear, and with orders to advance back to the front line, on the 3rd March we set off west on a twelve-day journey, eventually covering over 1,000 miles, before we encountered the enemy.

We moved like a giant column of ants across the desert. Sometimes it was hard going; rocky and strewn with large boulders and potholes everywhere. Sometimes we made good progress along roads and tracks, but mostly it was slow, going cross-country to avoid obstacles, through soft powdery sand with emergency low gear and four-wheel drive engaged. Sometimes the journey involved *driving carefully* down escarpments or quickly through wadis.

It was very well organised and planned; our reconnaissance troops had worked out the complete route we were going to take well before we set off. It was a long journey, undertaken with military precession, whilst observing very strict convoy discipline.

The journey took us through the Martabua Pass along the main coastal road and past Benghasi to Buergat, then through Gheddahia, Bendi Ulid, Tarhuna, Castel Benito and Suani Ben Adem. The whole route was well marked so that no one could get lost, with Battery signs at all junctions and at regular distances. There were Military Police, or *Provosts*, directing traffic; they ensured that units only moved at the allocated times to guarantee that everything ran smoothly.

The cook vehicles and ourselves were always at the head of the convoy, which meant that, by the time the whole convoy arrived at the night stop, or *harbour area*, the evening meals were being prepared and we had already established the air defences.

Theses harbours were located about 200 yards from the road in a marked area measuring approximately 300 square yards, which had been swept clear for mines. Whilst there was the obvious danger from mines if you left the safety of the harbour, the biggest problem we had was with the locals. They were slippery characters who would steal anything they could get their hands on. You had to always keep your kit strapped to a part of your body, otherwise it would go missing.

We moved at a slow and monotonous speed of ten miles per hour, and maintained a gap of forty yards between trucks, which was strictly enforced. We did stop every few hours for a ten-minute halt, enough to go to the toilet and stretch your legs, but we never wandered too far off the tracks for fear of mines. Once it was time to move again, we were each responsible for letting the vehicle behind know, and off we would go. We did have a longer stop at midday so we could have a cuppa char, some bully beef, and take on petrol and water. However, we had to man the Bren guns in the event of air attack every time we stopped. For the first part of the journey, we were allowed to use headlights at night, but once we reached Buaerat we adopted total 'lights-out' discipline on the move and in the night time harbours and reverted back to vehicle cooking.

I do remember stopping about seven miles past on the 5th March for rest and maintenance at a large oasis. We did some bartering with the local Arabs for luxuries like water melon and salad. An unhappy memory of that place was the hundreds of dead tortoises that had been crushed by our trucks and tanks.

We had to avoid many towns en route; these were out of bounds to troops, because they were so heavily mined. At first, minefields were well marked, but as we advanced the engineers were still clearing, and things became more hazardous.

It wasn't long before the vehicles started to feel the strain. As a rule, in the event that a vehicle broke down, if it could be towed it was; if not, it was pushed off the road and the crew would stay with the *crock* to wait for the mechanics who were following-up in the rear. We lost two mechanics en route when they went to an abandoned German half-track to salvage some spare parts, only to be killed by a booby-trap.

On the morning of the 14th we had reached our dispersal area four miles east of Ben Gardane near to the Matmata Hills. We had just dug our trenches and had a brew on the go. I could just make out the outline of Ben Gardane, and was thinking how peaceful it was, when suddenly the quiet of the afternoon was disturbed by a shrill whistle and we all dropped like tall grass under a scythe. I found myself face first in the sand with a bent cigarette in my mouth, acting like a new recruit. The shells exploded about half a mile from us, and we were laughing it off when more 88 shells came over us with a whistle. This time they were closer, and I got that all-too-familiar feeling, like someone placing an icy hand on your back, which let me know that this time they were meant for me. I dived for cover into my trench, with shell fragments buzzing over my head and the pressure from one of the explosions causing the sides of my trench to crumble in on me. There was lots of shouting and soon everyone was on the move. I jumped on the running board of the nearest truck and hung on as we bumped over the desert out of range of the enemy guns. We looked like something out of a Wild West show, tearing eastwards in clouds of dust. After about a mile we stopped, and everyone reunited themselves with their own crew and truck; thankfully everyone was accounted for, although one truck had hit an anti-personnel mine, injuring six gunners.

The following days were spent repairing the trucks after the long journey; the mechanics did an amazing job to keep them going. By this time, most of our vehicles had been kept on the road thanks to repairs using odd parts off vehicles belonging to eight different nations!

On the 17th, we were back in the open desert, this time following Sherman tanks sneaking south around the Matmata Mountains in support of the Second New Zealand Corps.

The Battle of the Mareth Line started on 20th March, with the Highland Division attacking 22 miles of defences on the eastern coastal flank, known as the Mareth Line. We were part of a mostly New Zealand force, which was sent south in an outflanking manoeuvre to attack the western flank; we passed through Wilder's Gap, Ksar Rhilane, Bir Soltane, and Plum Defile, before eventually arriving at El Hamma. The Battle did not start well; the Jocks met stiff resistance, and the enemy's coastal defences turned out to be almost impregnable. All was made worse by enemy air activity; planes attacked with an intensity not seen since El Alamein.

We continued northwards to an area about six miles south of El Hammer, in an attempt to completely encircle the enemy. This we eventually did, but then found ourselves facing a very angry and determined enemy force. We quickly deployed in all-round defensive positions as we were engaged by enemy tanks and infantry. They eventually counter-attacked and we became surrounded ourselves. They then placed an anti-tank screen to our south in some trees by an oasis, to prevent our break-out. We were cut off; ammunition was starting to run out and we were at the mercy of accurate heavy artillery, mortar, strafing by ME 210s, and bombing from JU 88s. They attacked us relentlessly for about two days.

Planes would suddenly appear from over the hills and came at us as low as the telegraph poles; they would head straight for us, and when they got within about 250 yards they opened fire. Sometimes, it happened so fast that you never saw them until they had passed by. When we did get enough warning, everybody went mad; in addition to the Ack-Acks, the Bren guns, rifles and pistols were all firing, with everyone shouting and swearing. Hurricanes were sometimes in action, but it was difficult to tell ours from theirs; we often fired at everything.

We heard General Montgomery announce on the BBC that "The attack is proceeding according to plan. A small unit is reported surrounded near the desert town of El Hamma." However, he was not concerned about the fact that the attacks in progress were expected to break through our defences in this sector. He may not have been concerned, but we damn well were!

One evening there had been a lull in the fighting; Jerry came over and dropped parachute flares in preparation for a bombing run. One of the lads decided that he wanted to salvage the silk parachute to send to his wife back home; regardless of the risk, he set off into the desert to collect it before anyone else could. The sight of this chap running and weaving around like a drunkard chasing the parachute as it got blown in one direction then another was hilarious, and was made even funnier when he fell into a pit or just stumbled. I laughed so much it hurt. I was not alone; the enemy were watching this too, and when he eventually caught his prize everyone cheered.

It was a terrifying time, but after an artillery bombardment you would often find groups of men completely entwined in the bottom of a depression or hole where they had taken shelter in peals of laughter for no particular reason. With this said, there was the time that I dived for cover to find the hole was actually a mortar pit; being surrounded by all that live ammo wasn't funny at the time! You could say that I nearly died laughing on more than one occasion.

One of my mates was badly hurt during a Stuka attack while lying in a slit trench which was far too shallow to be of any use. A bullet ripped through his upper thigh, smashing the bone. I went to his aid; he was conscious but in a state of shock and bleeding like mad. I stuffed a cigarette into his mouth and applied a tourniquet and a shell dressing over the gaping wound; this was difficult, as his leg was almost severed. I did the best I could; he was eventually evacuated to the field hospital, but later died.

Eventually, General Montgomery ordered the Tenth Corps to follow the route we had taken around the Matmata Hills to add its weight to our attack. At the same time, the Jocks were starting to make progress on the coast, and the Fourth Indian Division joined the battle and pushed through the hills.

On the 25th, we finally pushed our way out; the New Zealanders successfully attacked the high hills, and the following day we passed through enemy minefields and headed towards El Hamma. There were terrific tank battles going on, both in front and to our rear. The desert was so flat and visibility so good that you could see everything. Throughout the day we moved forward, passing many enemy tanks still burning, their dead crews lying in grotesque positions all around.

We also saw the familiar sight of surrendering troops at first light the next day, when approximately 700 Italians surrendered. The German troops did not give up so easily, but by the 29th March, we reached El Hamma; the enemy had evacuated the Mareth Line, and the battle was won.

18
Faster Than a Speeding Camel

We started the month of April 1943 in the area of the El Hamma Oasis in Tunisia, about twenty miles west of the ancient coastal town of Gabes; here we rested amongst the lush palm plantations, surrounded by hills and deep wadis. I remember the rocks were a light pink colour and changed shade every time it rained. It was a beautiful place, apart from all the killing of course.

Despite the enemy retreating, there was still a very effective rear-guard to deal with before the war in North Africa would be over. Even though the RAF was very active overhead, we would still get enemy bombers and fighter aircraft attacking us during the day and night. Added to this, with the enemy artillery occasionally shelling our positions, things were still very uncomfortable.

In the past, we would often *hold fire* when the RAF was operating in our area. However, because of the effectiveness and sheer volume of the enemy aircraft, we received orders to *take-care*; at this point, all the light and heavy Ack-Acks swung into action, with spotters doing their best to identify friendly aircraft in the crowded sky. We were constantly in operation and shot down several enemy aircraft almost every day.

One memorable incident happened during the late afternoon of the 6th April, when six ME 109 enemy fighters arrived at our location from the north. They had been trying to return to their base, flying very low and hugging the ground in the vain hope of avoiding our spitfires. Before they knew where they were, and too late to change direction, they fell into our gun sights as they passed close to our positions. By now we were very experienced, and so they didn't stand a chance; all the guns were swung into action, and we lay down a terrific barrage. Four of the planes were destroyed instantly, and the remaining two limped over a hill, full of holes, leaving smoke trails behind them.

By now, we were supporting Indian troops, and together we advanced northwards; we were constantly on the alert for an enemy counter-attack, but it never came. As we advanced, forward movement became increasingly difficult, for the same old reasons; too much traffic for the desert tracks to cope with, and the fact that the harsh terrain could only be navigated along set routes, which had been mined and booby-trapped.

Our main objective was to take the town of Mezzouna, which was still held by the enemy. It was here that we first encountered American forces from the First Army.

Whilst their arrival was a welcome sight, it was fraught with difficulty. We were both converging on each other from the same direction as the enemy had been; the colour and sight of unfamiliar makes of vehicles created confusion. It was difficult to tell the difference between friend and foe, so neither side dared to fire a shot out of fear that they might hit friendly troops.

Once the two Armies joined, the weight of force against the enemy was overwhelming, and they soon made their escape. We were quick to follow, but the ground was too rough for trucks to move at speed, and we were unable to keep up with the tanks. Not long afterwards, it started to rain again, and with all the mist, visibility was down to zero. We couldn't target anything even if we wanted to, and on the 10th we stopped for two days of essential maintenance.

On 12th April, news came through that the town of Sousse had been penetrated by the Eighth Army, while the First Army had entered the town of Kairouan. This was the news we had been waiting for. The planned pincer-movement had been a success, and our mission was over.

We knew that once the two armies joined, there was going to be a considerable amount of reorganisation, and that the role of the regiment would change. It didn't take long. Within a few days, the 1st Armoured Division were *lent* to the First Army, and a United States Army team arrived with paint spraying equipment and spent the day camouflaging our vehicles with the dark green paint used by the First Army. Before long, tanks were loaded onto transporters and we set off on the evening of the 17th for a long night march. We took the main road through Faid Pass, continuing the next day via Sbeittla and Le Kef, before eventually arriving at Aroussa railway station, where we assembled in a shady olive grove.

It was here that I received orders telling me that I would be transferred to the Sixteenth Heavy Anti-Aircraft Battery. The battery was established in the Baggush Box near Marsa Matruh, Egypt, in the area that I had been in ten months earlier, in June 1942. The Box was a fortress, built by hand at the beginning of the campaign to protect the main coastal route and the end of the western railway.

It took the better part of a week to get to Mersa Matruh. Three days' travelling by road to Tripoli was followed by a Canadian ferry directly into the Port at Mersa Matruh. We arrived in early May at a transit camp just outside Matruh, alongside the single line railway which went back to El Alamein.

At the time, there was a lot of confusion and uncertainty as the army reorganised itself and started to prepare for the next phase of the war — the invasion of Italy. Now that there were two armies in North Africa, it felt like they did not know what to do with us all. So, the army did what it was best at, and sent us to a godawful spot in the desert to dig holes and then guard them. It was not yet high summer, but the temperatures were torrid and we found ourselves posted too far away from the coast to benefit from the cooling wind that came in off the Mediterranean Sea. This also meant we were too far away for the much-enjoyed frequent bathing parties. But worse still, we were back on chlorinated water, tinned beef, and anti-scorbutic vitamin C tablets. I knew from experience that this area would become hell in the winter once the annual deluge started. It would turn rapidly into a sea of mud and all the tent pits would become ponds with half submerged bell tents. I just hoped that we would be long gone before winter arrived.

We settled into a comfortable but familiar routine. I adopted a chameleon as a pet, which I fed on a readily available diet of flies. I also had a prize black scorpion — an evil little thing with a terrible sting, which fought daily. It was a favourite gambling activity which involved making a fighting ring by pouring petrol on the ground and setting it alight, then letting several scorpions fight against each other. The winnings kept me well supplied with cigarettes for some considerable time, before the inevitable happened and he was defeated.

A major hazard at the time was unexploded bombs which were still lying around. For years, the Italians had dropped AR-4 booby-trap bombs all over the place. Most were destroyed soon after they had been dropped, but some had been missed and, unfortunately, we would occasionally come across one of these devices when out looking for scorpions. Although the temptation to walk straight past was overwhelming, you had to deal with them before they killed someone. We called them *thermos bombs* because they looked just like a thermos flask. They were horrible things, with sensitive motion-detection fuses which, if they went off, would kill anything within fifty feet. There were two methods of dealing with these devils; my preferred method was to shoot at them from a very safe distance, with a heavy machine-gun until they exploded. The one which was preferred by the army was to tie a long piece of string to the bomb and then give it a jerk from a safe distance.

I learnt a valuable lesson when one of my mates made two mistakes. Firstly, he got too close to the device and secondly he thought that lying in a shallow depression rather than digging a hole would provide adequate protection when it went off. He was wrong, and spent the rest of the day with the medical officer getting small fragments of shell casing removed from his backside. He was also unable to sit down without a cushion for several weeks afterwards.

A funny thing happened one day, whilst I was on guard duty at one of the forward positions. It had been a long and boring day in stifling heat when, out of the haze, coming straight towards my post was a small camel train of Bedouins. As they approached, I ordered them to 'halt', which they did. It was obvious that they were friendly, and as they were about to continue their journey, I noticed that one of the elders had an ancient muzzle-loading flintlock rifle called a *banduq jauhardar* slung over his back. It was a strange looking weapon, with a fish tail stock and beautifully decorated all over. "I will give you a bag of tea, if you let me fire the gun?" I said.

The trade was soon agreed, and with much manipulation the elder loaded the antique rifle. I soon discovered that the trigger did not have a safety guard and was very sensitive to the touch; it had what we called a *hair trigger*. Before I was able to take a proper aim there was an almighty bang and a cloud of smoke. I heard a scream, and as the smoke cleared I could see that I had startled a camel a short distance away. The scream came from a poor Arab boy who had been thrown off his beast. Luckily, he landed in soft sand, which was a miracle as the ground was generally hard and rocky. The camel then shot off into the desert at speed towards a minefield, throwing off all the boy's belongings on its way. Fortunately, it stopped before the minefield and remained unhurt.

"*Every inch of the desert had been touched in some way by the war. The sand was full of shrapnel and broken slices of metal from countless high explosive shells, bombs and bullets, which had fallen amongst our trenches and the now rusting barbed wire.*"

"*When the sandstorms came, they would shift enough sand to expose guns and vehicles from previous battles and the macabre sight of half submerged skeletons of the fallen from both sides.*"

19
The Eighth Army Chatter

The Eighth Army had a language all of its own. It mostly involved the use of swear words, but it also included an interesting mixture of slang words from back home, such as 'bacca', for tobacco, 'blimey', which was short for 'gorblimey', which was itself short for 'God blind me'. Added to this, 'clobber' referred to our uniform or clothing, and the word 'daisy-roots' was slang for boots. Sometimes, words or phrases came about locally, like 'Jerrican' for the German petrol can, and ' cooker' for the petrol cooker; a lavatory was called a 'desert lily'.

We even adopted words from other nations. The South African troops used the word 'kip', which originates from the Danish word for bed; this became a commonly-used word for sleep.

When I first arrived in North Africa, a lot of words and phrases that soldiers commonly used had their origins in India. This was not unsurprising, as that is where many of the soldiers had recently served before joining the campaign. Some of those Hindu words we used I still hear today. Words like 'char', which means tea, and 'dekko', from the word *deckna'*, meaning to have a look; I also often hear 'pukka', which means first-class.

As we traversed across North Africa, we began using Egyptian, Libyan and Persian words like 'cushy', meaning easy, and eventually all conversations were enriched with

Arabic. Although 'char' was always popular, the Arabic word 'shai' was also used, as was 'bint', which means girl. Some memorable sayings included 'marleesh', meaning it does not matter, 'bar din', meaning later, 'alakeefic', meaning I don't care, and 'musdh kye-ee', which meant no good. No one would ask for the time in English; it was always "sar kam da watti?"

Sometimes it would be a combination; 'shufti' means look, so we would say "let's go and have a shufti." The word for number one is 'wha-hid', and for road is 'sharia'. So, "Let's have one for the road," became "let's have wha-hid more for the sharia."

We even had our own catch phrases, such as "Just the job" if things were going well, and "There's no future in this," when things weren't going our way. "I'm going to the NAAFI for lemonade and buns," was a phrase often used, and meant returning to camp for fuel and resupply. Back home we were 'BBLs' full of beef, beer, and lust.

But not all the words we used were respectful, especially when describing people. It was common to call someone of mixed British and Indian race, 'chee-chee'. A derogatory term for the locals was 'WOG', an acronym for Working On Government Service; this came from a term given to the clerical 'effendi' class by Evelyn Baring, who was the British, Egypt, Controller-General in 1877. It started off innocently enough, but over the years changed to something offensive. Everything that was Egyptian was preceded by the acronym, but it was generally meant abusively.

We were called 'Pom' or 'Pommie' by Australian and New Zealand soldiers. I think this came from the word 'pomade', which was a greasy or waxy substance that we used to style our hair at the time. I heard other explanations; one was the Australian rhyming slang, similar to our cockney slang for an immigrant, which was 'Jimmy-Grant'; this, in turn, evolved into 'pomegranate'. Another was that when we arrived in Africa our fair skin soon turned the colour of a pomegranate. There were also acronyms such as 'POME', which came from Prisoner Of Mother England, and 'POHMS', from prisoner Of Her Majesty's Service. It was probably a mixture of all of them.

The Americans called us 'Limeys'. Apparently, 'lime-juicer' had been slang for a British sailor. It had something to do the Royal Navy adding lime juice to the sailors' daily ration to prevent scurvy. The expression stuck and was commonly used to describe all the British.

We were also called *Tommies* by Commonwealth troops and the Germans — a term that became popular in World War One. Its origin is interesting; the name 'Atkins' was made famous by the Duke of Wellington in 1794 when, after the Battle of Boxtel, he commended the bravery of Private Thomas Atkins from the Thirty-third Regiment of Foot, who was named as the best man-at-arms during the fierce engagement. He was reported as saying, "It's all right, sir. It's all in a day's work" just before he died.

Soon afterwards, in the 1800s, the name 'Tommy Atkins' became a fictitious name used in pay books and on army registration forms to illustrate how they should be filled in. It changed after WW1, and the name 'George Bull, Fusilier No.1973' was used instead.

In 1892, Rudyard Kipling wrote a poem called *Tommy* and in the following year Henry Hamilton wrote a popular music hall song, *Private Tommy Atkins.*

So Tommy was a well-established label and Tommies we were as well as being Desert Rats.

20
On the Lights

At that stage of the war, things were beginning to look a little brighter. The Germans had been beaten in North Africa, American troops were arriving in numbers, and the RAF was bombing Germany almost on a nightly basis. In the Far East, things were not as good. The Japanese had overrun Malaya and it seemed that my options were to remain in North Africa, join the crusade into Italy, or head for the Far East to fight the Japanese.

Until someone made a decision on my destiny, I was guarding the desert and about to undergo extensive training as part of the preparation for the allied invasion of Italy.

I was in no rush to go anywhere, as I was completely exhausted both mentally and physically. Today, I would have been diagnosed with Post Traumatic Stress Disorder (PTSD), which in those days was known as *battle exhaustion*. When I eventually got to sleep, I would be woken by terrifying nightmares. I was listless, depressed and found it hard to make close friends.

It was thought that a soldier could tolerate just over a year of constant action before becoming non-functional. I had been in almost constant combat since May the previous year, and although I didn't know it at the time, I had been earmarked for non-combatant duties.

In June 1943, I was transferred from Sixteenth Brigade to the 195th Light Anti-Aircraft Battery, Fifty-Second Light Anti-Aircraft Regiment, which was under the command of the Eighteenth Anti-Aircraft Brigade. The brigade was responsible for providing air cover, all the way from Mersa Matruh eastwards to the Suez Canal, with its headquarters in Alexandria.

The Fifty-Second was a very prestigious regiment. It had been in France and Belgium in 1939, supporting the withdrawal of troops in May and June 1940, on the beaches at Dunkirk. The regiment was evacuated along with 340,000 other troops, but they had to leave their equipment behind. Once back in England, they had a short three-month respite in the North Midlands before being sent to join the Mediterranean Expeditionary Force (MEF) in September. They were then engaged with the defence of Greece in 1941 and were amongst the last troops to be evacuated from the Corinth Canal, where they were deployed to support the withdrawal of our troops. They continued retreating south, where they ended up defending the airfields around Argos in Crete, assisting the New Zealanders during their escape along the coast. They were eventually evacuated, but suffered considerable losses; only four officers and ninety men escaped out of just over 200 troops.

On the 5th June 1943, I joined the regiment at Port Said, a day after they had arrived from Tabruk. I became a member of A Troop, 195th LAA Battery, and I was stationed alongside gunners from 100th LAA Battery on the eastern side of the Suez Canal.

It was a very quiet period for us; there was the occasional enemy JU86P flying overhead on reconnaissance missions, but they flew at forty-five thousand feet, so were well out of range of our guns. More often than not, they were intercepted by a fighter patrol and destroyed. There was also the occasional JU88 bomber flying low enough to have a go at, but they were en route to or from Alexandria, and avoided us as best they could.

We would rotate between the guns and our Battery Headquarters, which was situated on the western side of the Suez Canal, on the western outskirts of the town, just past the sports stadium on the main road to Damietta.

It was a pleasant enough place, and was very close to the sea, which was great for swimming. There was even a NAFFI hut where we could get beer, and because the RAF's fighter defence headquarters were very nearby there was the welcome distraction of the occasional dance night with the Women's Auxiliary Air Force (WAAF).

The HQ was right next to the local Muslim Cemetery and the WW1 War Cemetery, now the site of a Commonwealth War Grave cemetery. The cemetery was already pretty full with those killed at Gallipoli and at sea during WW1. We would often get local funeral processions passing by the camp. These were very dignified affairs, occasionally accompanied by women relatives wailing. There were also a number of service burials when I was there, and I went to two funerals for artillery lads — Gunner John White, Twenty-Eighth Heavy Anti-Aircraft Battery, who came from Shropshire, and Arthur Atkins, who was with the 305th Search Light Battery.

One day, a couple of us were asked to help carry the coffin of a local British lady who had died in a car accident. She had been in Egypt with her husband, who was a port customs officer, when her car was hit by an army truck.

June to July was a period of constant changes; there were lots of visits and inspections, and all the officers seemed to be getting promoted and posted to other units. We had visits from the General Officer Commanding (GOC) anti-aircraft in the Middle East, Major General Pollock, and our Brigade Commander Brigadier Wilson. We were also joined briefly by 222/37 LAA battery, who stayed with us for only a week before moving on, along with our Commanding Officer, Lt. Col. Chaytor, who was replaced by Lt. Col. Darrell-Browning. It was a very boring time, with nothing to do but sit around all day and work on our defensive positions.

There were lots of locals employed in constructing the defensive positions, off-loading ships and moving supplies, which was great because it meant we did not have to dig, shift heavy loads, or mess about with barbed wire. However, there were a few downsides. One was that they would go to the toilet wherever they wanted, refusing to use the facilities provided. This meant, apart from there being even more flies, that you were constantly watching where you stepped.

The local workers would be organised into small groups led by a Headman or *Rais,* but supervised by one of our sergeants. We were under strict orders not to use force to coax them into work, which was difficult, as they were often very lazy, doing the bare minimum of work. Despite the threat of severe discipline if we hit any of the locals, the toe of an army boot was occasionally applied as an incentive to work. On one occasion, the sergeant gave a regular work dodger a kick up the backside, which resulted in the individual falling theatrically to the ground pretending to die. This led to the whole work party downing tools to gather around their fallen brother. The *corpse* was then taken by his grieving friends to the Regimental Aid Post and presented to the medical officer, Captain Chambers. The Officer suddenly produced a huge hypodermic syringe with the largest needle I had ever seen. At this point, the corpse suddenly came to life and burst out of the aid post, as fast as his legs could carry him.

I had a short respite from the monotony for two weeks at the end of June, when I was sent to the Radar School just outside Cairo for familiarisation on the latest American-made equipment. It was a bit of a shock, as it was the first time I had seen radar since arriving in Egypt and being put straight onto the guns.

I returned to the unit on the 1st July. In just two weeks, the mood in camp had changed, and because there was now an expectation that we would soon be mobilised, all the training took on a more realistic feel. Training also focused on improving standards in discipline and turnout, which caused considerable consternation because the Eighth Army had adopted its own particular style, which conflicted with the traditional spit and polish which the regular army now required.

So, every day started after stand-to and breakfast with physical training which we did first before it got too hot. This was followed by fifteen minutes of foot drills, marching up and down and saluting each other. Soon after that we undertook a half hour gun drill, practicing changing barrels, lining up the gun and misfire actions. By then it was lunch, and the hottest part of the day, so we would just lounge around our guns. When it cooled down in the afternoon we would undertake route marches or field firing.

We had to shine all the brass on webbing belts, cap badges and our tunic buttons, just like in basic training. There was weekly gas mask training and constant *plane alert* drills, when everyone had to adopt all around spotter duties. There was an obsession with ensuring that the vehicles were serviceable and ready to move at any time. One officer would have us checking the tyre pressures two or three times a day. We also underwent a two-day field exercise which involved driving into the middle of nowhere for half a day to a makeshift firing rage, firing the gun briefly, then returning to where we had started. There was also a programme of lectures and specialist courses for medics, signallers, drivers and radar operators.

Tension increased when we received orders that the number of invasion shipping convoys was about to increase around the port, and that we should expect the enemy to attack. Additional troops were sent into the area and we were joined by the 149/27 Anti-Aircraft Regiment and by the evening of the 3rd July everyone was in position to receive the fleet.

On the 14th July, I was ordered to go on spotter duty by my sergeant shortly after returning from morning PT. The general rule was that the morning spotter did not do PT because it would not leave enough time to get changed and get to the post to relieve the shift at 10 a.m. so I told him to "Get stuffed."

Unfortunately, an officer overheard me and I soon found myself in front of the CO; I was fined fourteen days' pay for disobeying a lawful command. It was silly, because everyone knew that the sergeant was wrong, but they were enforcing discipline, and I was just in the wrong place at the wrong time. Two days later, I was promoted to Lance Bombardier, which made a mockery of the whole incident.

The 27th July was my real birthday and I celebrated with a bowl of hot stew and a beer. My father had sent me a parcel which I had received a week earlier, but I kept it safe until the day, so I would have something to unwrap. He had sent me a watch, which was treasured by me at the time.

Everything changed rapidly when, on the 6th August, the CO was ordered to travel to headquarters in Cairo. It was supposed to be a secret, but his departure was soon noticed and the rumours of mobilisation began. We did not have to wait too long; on the 9th, we received orders that we would be moving-out soon.

During the day of the 11th August, our position was relieved by 15/45 Battery. We handed over the guns and stores, and that evening, under the cover of darkness, we crossed the canal by ferry and concentrated near to the HQ.

At first light, the regiment moved first to Mena and then onto the transit camp at Amarya. From there, we travelled 270 miles to Alexandria. We moved in a convoy of forty-six trucks, driving across mile after mile of *sweet Fanny Adams* in a dust cloud, over rough ground in terrible heat. Strict convoy discipline was enforced, which included no tail-gate riding; despite being dangerous, it was the only real escape from the heat and dust.

When we eventually reached Alexandria we were all confined to our vehicles. This was so no one could take a quick trip into Alex and end-up missing the boat. We were separated from our kit bags, which were loaded separately and fumigated for lice. We were then issued with mosquito cream and mepacrine hydrochloride tablets for *gippy tummy*.

We eventually boarded the Polish troop ship 'Sobieski' and the regiment set sail in convoy on the 18th. We arrived at Tripoli on the 22nd, where we disembarked and made our way to No.201 Rest Camp, under the command of the Twelfth Anti-Aircraft Brigade.

It was called a rest camp, but it was far from it! It had been transformed into a mini garrison and its purpose was to intensively train troops in preparation for the invasion of Italy. Out went the *bull shit*, and we concentrated on combat training; fitness was a priority, with route marches top of the agenda. Everyone had to be able to swim, and we learnt hand-to-hand fighting techniques, as well as practicing mine-laying and running gun drills.

We were also taught how to scramble up nets to get on and off ships. This involved wading out to boats located offshore whilst trying to avoid falling into a hole and getting submerged. Once you eventually reached the ship, soaking wet, there was the difficult task of trying to scale a sagging rope net whilst the ship was swaying. More often than not, you would be left hanging upside down, or worse, lose your footing and end-up with both legs astride the netting and your *balls* where your tonsils should be!

It was during this period that they were looking for volunteers to become dispatch riders. I already had some experience with motorbikes, having owned one before the war. Added to this, I had been up, down and across North Africa, meaning I had plenty of knowledge of the local terrain. I never hesitated in volunteering, and shortly afterwards, I was issued with orders to make my way to the headquarters of the Eighteenth Anti-Aircraft Brigade, 121 Sharia Tigran Pasha in Alexandria. On the 14th September 1943, I stood dockside and waved off 116 officers and men of 195th Battery as they headed for Italy.

I returned by boat to Alexandria with the Ninety-fourth HAA, arriving sometime around the 20th September. I was then sent to No.1 Anti-Aircraft Camp at Deir el-Bahri to train as a dispatch rider. The camp was located close to the temple of Queen Hatshepsut and the famous Valley of the Kings.

One day, a German Luftwaffe pilot appeared at our camp shortly after we had shot him down. It was not long before we were all crowded around his bed asking him all sorts of questions. Now, only an hour earlier we had been intent on killing him and calling him every filthy name under the sun! But, there we were clustered around like old pals instead of enemies.

He explained how he had been photographing our positions and got too close when he ran into our barrages, damaging his wing sending his plane crashing to the ground. He had escaped death by bailing out over our lines, where he had been picked up by our men, slightly injured during the landing and been brought to our camp to see the MO. We were laughing and cheering at the German's gutteral description of the event and our success in shooting him down. Then, in came a medical orderly, who had never been anywhere near the front line, and certainly never seen any fighting. At the sight of us making a fuss of the German, he turned to us and shouted, "You should be ashamed of yourselves, he was killing your mates a day ago!" He was met with a chorus of abuse from us and told to "Go and get stuffed!"

I often think of that event and the thoughts and actions of British soldiers. The German regular troops at the front fought with chivalry as well as skill and for that were respected. There was a comradeship with the men that tried to kill you and that you tried to kill, I guess because they were enduring the same hardships and experience as ourselves.

21
Read All About It

Knowing what was going on was very important to us all; not knowing would cause even more rumours to fly around than usual. So, we would listen to the radio whenever we could, or read any scrap of news or magazine to find out what was going on both at home, and on other battle-fronts.

The *airgraphs*, or letters from home, were the most eagerly anticipated of arrivals every day. Whenever a truck would arrive, everyone watched to see if any mailbags were thrown off; if they were, the whole mood would lift. It is difficult to express how important getting a letter from home was for morale. An airgraph was a method used to send letters, and involved writing a message on a special form which was then photographed onto microfilm. The microfilm was flown to its destination; the message was then developed back into a full-size letter and posted to the recipient. This method kept down the transportation weight, and you would get letters from England within two weeks of them being sent.

For up-to-date news, we relied on locally-produced newspapers. As well as the formal printed civilian newspapers, there were lots of home-made military-magazines. These were often short-lived, and some were even written and printed within the range of enemy guns. A few of those which lasted for quite a while were an RAF paper called *Gen*, which was RAF slang for general information. The Tankies had one that they called *Parade Crusader*, and there was a Cairo-edited and printed magazine called *Personal*

Landscape. The first soldier's newspaper was the *Allied Post*, which was printed by three men on a small captured German printing press, with its illustration blocks cut out of wood using razor blades.

There was a military newspaper called the *Eighth Army News*, which you could say was closer to a proper newspaper than any of the others. The *Eighth Army News* started life in a tent nicknamed *Fleet Street* around June 1942. It was the daily bulletin of news, mostly a condensed version of the BBC News being produced for Montgomery at the time. Soon, other snippets and stories were added from the battle-front and from publicity officers. The distribution list quickly grew, and very soon it received official recognition and became broadly circulated across North Africa. It then moved out of its tent and into purpose-built lorries, and became the Field Publicity Unit.

The newspapers were delivered by clerks in a jeep, who acted as newspaper boys. But the jeep often broke down, and if our destination for the day took in a scheduled drop-off, we would strap a bundle of papers to the back of the bike and deliver them. This was never seen as a chore; we all knew what it meant to the troops to get something to read, and we always received a warm welcome wherever we delivered them.

There were of course local civilian-published newspapers, mostly in French, but some in English, which also found their way out into the desert. There was a daily one called *La Bourse Egyptienne*, which cost half a piastre. It was meant for circulation amongst the French-speaking residents of Cairo and Alexandria. You would often hear the Egyptian newsboys standing on street corners shouting, "La Bourse!" Even though I don't speak French, it carried up-to-date pictures which made it a favourite read along with another large weekly picture paper, again in French, but also very popular. The same publishers also produced the *Egyptian Mail* and the *Egyptian Gazette*; both were in English and carried the same stories, but for some reason it was much harder to get a copy. The *Egyptian Mail* would come out in the morning, but it often lacked the benefits of English spelling and layout checks; consequently, there were often a fair number of howlers in the text, which was always funny.

The Gazette, on the other hand, was published in the evening, often having had the luxury of being edited properly. It also had a column which was popular with the troops, called *Passing By*; this was written by an American redhead called Miss Spencer Brocke. The paper cost one piastre, and was sold in Cairo and Alexandria; I would often grab several copies to sell and trade on my travels.

One other paper worthy of a mention was the *Al-Ahram* which, although printed in Arabic, often had some great pictures and was delivered throughout North Africa. There was also *The War Illustrated*, which was mainly produced for home consumption, but found its way to North Africa. It was very popular because, unlike the local papers, there were articles from battle-fronts all over the world, and for all arms of the service.

All this media activity shouldn't really have come as a surprise given that North Africa was full of talented writers and skilled newspapermen and women drafted to fight the war. Some were in rest camps convalescing following battle field injuries; bored and looking for something to do and would inevitably find themselves drawn towards the publishing houses.

The source for most stories was an official spokesman, nicknamed *The Voice of Cairo*, who gave daily press conferences at GHQ Cairo. Before being published, all material had to be censored by the army, navy, the RAF, and even the Egyptian government. At the beginning of the North African campaign, correspondents weren't allowed anywhere near the front line. This meant the only source was the daily briefings, and reporters complained that things were being covered up.

A very famous journalist at the time was Richard Dimbleby. He was a BBC Radio correspondent who we would often hear on the radio at night, and who was with us at El Alamein. He complained, at the highest level, that it was wrong that he wasn't able to use information received from sources other than GHQ. For his troubles, he was returned to England. He was soon back reporting though, and landed with the troops in Normandy on D-Day; he even flew raids with the RAF as an observer and reported the horrors at the Nazi concentration camp Belsen. I used to watch him after the war on television when he hosted the TV programme *Panorama* before his death in 1965.

Things changed when Montgomery arrived, because he saw the value of publicity and allowed more access to the battlefields for reporters. This came with a price; the field journalists were always escorted by military officers. The cushy job of escorting the press seemed to be given to nobility, or those that had been at school with the commanders of the armed forces. This did benefit the journalists, as it gave them easy access to higher ranking officials, but the military authorities still introduced strict controls on what could and could not be released.

The Field Publicity Unit continued to grow and was allowed to operate more freely than the escorted print journalists. Each division and brigade had a combat cameraman assigned to it. They all carried the rank of sergeant, which at first caused problems, as they often needed to approach officers, who had little time for non-commissioned officers. Montgomery intervened and eventually they became more accepted. I would often take cameramen to various locations on the back of the bike whenever their jeep broke down.

Not so popular were a bunch of army film photographers called *Chet's Circus*. In charge was a sergeant and former Fleet Street photographer called Chetwyn. He and his team spent most of the time in the rear areas filming reconstruction battle scenes. These reconstructions would find themselves on news reels being shown in cinemas back home, and even to us. Whenever they were shown, they were greeted by jeers and booing from those who had actually been there, for being fake.

It's true to say that most of those famous combat photographs showing us fighting in the western desert were fakes. A famous one of a chap storming an enemy position was, in fact, taken outside the cookhouse at the Australian Division's rear Headquarters. There were many others, reproduced for the sake of audience expectations. The production of these fabricated images was often supported by the army, who provided troops, damaged tanks and even engineers to make explosions. I guess they needed to show people what was going on, and since it's impossible for cameramen to be everywhere at once and in the thick of battle, reconstructions were inevitable.

Women were not allowed at the battle-front. However, a female reporter called Eve Curie, the daughter of the famous French scientist, Marie Curie, changed all that with the help of Winston Churchill's son Randolph.

In 1939, Eve was the head of the Feminine Division of the French Information Commission (Commissaire Général à l'information), when the Germans invaded France. She fled to England, where she joined the Free French Forces of General Charles de Gaulle. Between November 1941 and April 1942, Eve found herself in Cairo where she met Randolph Churchill, who was serving with the Fourth Queen's Own Hussars and later with the Special Air Service. With his help, Eve travelled as a war correspondent along the front line, just prior to the Battle of Gazala. It was short lived. One reason given was the poor sanitary arrangements. Being so basic and public meant that, when she arrived, everyone stopped going to the toilet. It was said that Randolph had to drive Eve several miles into the desert and turn his back when she needed to go!

Eve later volunteered for the Women's Medical Corps of the Free French Army's First Division and took part in the Italian Campaign. On the 15th August 1944, she took part in Operation Dragoon, the invasion of Southern France. After the war, she was decorated with the Croix de Guerre for her services.

"Newspapers were precious and rare commodities, they often found themselves pinned onto purpose-built notice boards so everyone could read them. Afterwards, they were eagerly recycled as toilet paper or as firelighters..."

22

Dispatch Rider

"How do you spot a happy dispatch rider..."
"... He has squashed flies on his teeth!"

In September 1943, Eighteenth Brigade Headquarters acquired five BSA M20 motorbikes and a dispatch rider squad was formed. Along with four others, in early October I embarked on six weeks of instruction at Deir el-Bahri on how to ride a motorbike and carry out the duties of a 'Don-R' or 'Dog-Roger', from words used in the phonetic alphabet. We were also known amongst some comedians as 'Dumb Rogers, 'Dog Robbers' or 'Dumb Russians'.

We got our bikes and tool kits issued on the first day, and spent the next few days listening to lectures on all the engine parts and how to maintain and repair them. We took them apart and put them back together again, so we knew them inside and out. We also had instruction on how to direct traffic and set routes for convoys, as well as how to read maps and obey dispatch rider etiquette; this basically involved knowing how to keep a record of the sender and receiver of messages, security, and how to destroy documents, to prevent them falling into enemy hands.

The first hands-on lesson was how to hold-up your motorcycle without letting it fall over; later, and just as importantly, we learnt how to fall off without hurting ourselves. After we had mastered kick-starting the bike and rattled our shins too many times to remember, we rode around and around a makeshift course made from rocks on the parade square. Once we had mastered the course, we set-off into the wilderness to learn how to control these beasts over rough terrain. Soon, we were covering greater and greater distances, familiarising ourselves with all the different camps we would later be visiting as dispatch riders.

Brigadier Morton was in command of Eighteenth Brigade and the primary role of most of the regiments was the defence of Alexandria and Cairo. So, we spent a lot of time learning how to navigate ourselves around the busy cities and routes between the Artillery Headquarters in Alexandria, and the Army General Headquarters in Garden City, Cairo. We also visited the Heavy Brigades at Aboukir and Wardian, and the Light Batteries east of Cairo, in Almaza and in Heliopolis. We were soon very familiar with the all the roads and, most importantly, the hotels where we could ring the doorbell and beg for a bed, a bath, and a shot of whisky any time of the day or night.

Our training trips would often pass through Quassassin, which was one of the largest transit camps in Egypt and slightly north of my favourite city, Ismailia, where we would stop to get fuel and rest. Ismaïlia, 'the City of Beauty and Enchantment', is located on the west bank of the Suez Canal by Lake Timsah. Whenever we could, we would often stop-over in the city and go to my favourite club, the Cocoanut Grove Casino, which was close to the marina.

On one occasion, we went to the cinema and watched a film called *40,000 Horsemen*, about the Australian and New Zealand Anzac Cavalry in the Sinai desert during WW1. The opponents were the same; it was just a different time and type of transport! It was a rowdy affair with cheering and whistling throughout, especially from the *Mad Bushmen* — the members of the audience who were from *down under*. We laughed at their antics throughout, and it still makes me smile when I remember that evening. I also recall a popular saying which came from that film:

> *"The torch you threw us we caught*
> *And our hands will hold it high.*
> *Its glorious light will never die!"*

We soon started to supplement our uniforms, 'in the Eighth Army way', with vital non-issue equipment. We had adopted a 'whatever works' ethic during Montgomery's command, but unfortunately change was in the air for the army, and uniform discipline was starting to take effect. Fortunately for us, we kept our distance from the mainstream troops and were able to keep up the tradition of scrounging. The most important new addition to my kit was a silk scarf to go around my neck. Riding a bike involves lots of neck movement, and with your neck rubbing against your shirt, this soon becomes unbearably uncomfortable. So, just like the early aviators, we would buy brightly-coloured neckerchiefs whenever we could.

I complimented my tool kit with some additional bits and pieces; an assortment of different screwdrivers, an Italian grease gun, and a German adjustable wrench. I knew from bitter experience that there was no guarantee where we would end-up during the day, or when or where we would get our next meal. I always made sure I had some basic rations tucked away on the bike. I had a few cans of beans which I kept near the engine so they would be warm when I needed them. I also had tins of bully beef, American bacon rashers, fruit, condensed milk, a few white potatoes, and a loaf of bread. I used my spare socks as storage containers; I filled one with loose tea, and the other with sugar.

At night, we would clean the bikes, repair our kit, and try and dry out our riding boots, which would fill with water every time it rained.

On Fridays, we were tested on what we had learnt during the week. Failure would mean being returned to our units, so it was very important to pass. You would also be returned to your unit if you failed to turn-up for parade every morning sober and properly dressed (SPD).

On one occasion, the instructor led us on a *swan-out* into the desert. We swanned down a wadi right through an infantry platoon who were practicing lobbing live hand grenades. No casualties, thankfully, and no laxatives needed for a couple of days!

We did get a few casualties, mostly from falling off the bike; there were no broken limbs, but a few nasty burns from the exhausts. We soon learnt that it was better to fling yourself away from a falling bike and risk a broken arm rather than getting your leg trapped under the bike next to the exhaust.

Our bikes were always breaking down, mainly due to the sandy conditions. The mechanics did fit extra filters, but the sand still got into the engine and the pistons were constantly being replaced. But that was only part of the problem; the pistons would go *out of round*, bulging and becoming distorted in the Mediterranean heat whilst sitting in boxes in the store. This should not have happened but it did; apparently, all the rubbish scrap metal being collected back home, including pots, pans and bits of old garden fence, was given to BSA who, in turn, ended up turning out grotty parts. To make things worse, mechanics then bored out the cast-iron cylinders to fit the new distorted pistons.

Another common occurrence would be a broken drive-chain. This was a messy job, and involved putting a spare link onto an oily chain in the heat or in the rain. It never happened near anywhere comfortable. You would push the bike off the road to fix it and have to listen to the cries of abuse from passing trucks. I soon got the hang of it, and could repair a chain in about fifteen minutes. A quick clean down using a rag dipped into the petrol tank, and I would be back on the road again.

Often too there would be an electrical short in the bike's wiring; a trick I learnt which allowed me to locate the problem was to put a nail where the fuse was and the short would start to smoke. Hopefully you would spot the smoke before it caught fire, fix the problem, and be on your way!

Soon the course was over; we all passed with flying colours and were granted fourteen days' leave. With a month's pay and two days' rations, we set off for the bright lights of Cairo the next morning.

23
Earnest John Pattinson

It was mid-November 1943; normally it would be a struggle to get out of a warm sleeping bag to be greeted by the cold winter morning frost. But not this time; I sprang out of bed eager to leave the training camp and get on the early 9 a.m. train leaving Luxor for Cairo — a journey north of nearly 400 miles. I, along with the others on the dispatch riders course, had two weeks' leave, with orders to report to our Artillery Headquarters in Alexandria on the 1st December. My plan was to spend my entire leave in Cairo, where I was going to meet up with my brother Earnest.

Luxor railway station was a scene of utter chaos, typical of any transit point. The whole station was teeming with people, all shouting instructions to each other with no noticeable effect. Our first job was to fight our way onto the train with all our worldly belongings and secure a first-rate spot, ideally as far away from the toilet as possible. It was better to be one of those in the queue, rather than trying to live alongside the stench and all the pushing and shoving that went on.

There were traders everywhere selling tea, sweets, spices, fruit, fly-whisks, razor blades and dirty *girly* magazines called *Zip Laffs*, *Wam* and *Saucy Snips*. I would avoid buying anything that had been washed in the local water, as you were guaranteed to get dysentery or cholera, or both. By now, I had mastered the best technique for dealing with vendors who would shove their stock through the windows at me; I would simply swear at them in Arabic. They took little or no offence at the insults, as it was part and parcel of dealing with British soldiers.

Whenever the train stopped, which was often, a brew-up was called for. There was a readily-available source of hot water from a release tap below the engine boiler. We would take it in turns to scavenge hot water and once the train stopped there would be a mad rush to the front of the carriage. When it was my turn, I made it to the front first to be greeted by an unhappy driver and crew. They rained down curses and lumps of coal, but I had had worse thrown at me in the past, and would not be denied a cuppa char.

At one stop, a trader came on board the train selling watches. They looked genuine enough; he even removed the back of a watch to show the quality of the movement. One of the lads bought a watch from him; shortly after, he was unable to get the watch to work, and it became clear he had been sold a fake. A few of the lads went off to look for him and eventually found him a few carriages further down trying to sell watches to some other soldiers. He was confronted, and after confessing to his wrongdoing, found his stock of watches hurled out of the train window. He was kept captive until the train had travelled a further 100 or so miles before he was allowed off. I have often wondered how long it took him to get back home.

During the previous month I had travelled in and out of Cairo on familiarisation training on several occasions. But I had never stopped overnight or explored the city, other than to get to know the best routes. The last time we had been in the city, knowing we would be coming back we made reservations at the service club, Talbot House, on Sharia Soliman Pasha. It was also known as the TOC-H; TOC being the WW1 signal language for the letter T, and H being short for House. Talbot House had been known as TOC-H since it was first founded in Belgium during WW1. Ever since then, whenever the Christian movement opened branches throughout the world, they adopted the same name.

We arrived in Cairo later that evening, and first made our way to the barracks close to the station to hand in our weapons before making the short walk to the hostel.

The next morning, I went to the barber shop for a shave, shampoo, haircut, and friction massage. I then went down to the local tailors to buy some corduroy trousers. I found a shop selling radar operator qualification badges in army brown rather than the issue RAF blue ones, and fixed one to my uniform. We all promoted ourselves to the rank of sergeant, as that would guarantee us better service in the bars. On one occasion, a chap promoted himself to major, and swaggered around the officer's mess for the duration of his leave without getting caught.

By now it had become routine to rotate front-line units at regular intervals, with some form of rest and relaxation. This meant that, every six months or so, soldiers would get a four or five-day pass with a choice of going into Cairo or Alexandria. The average soldier would try and cram every indulgence he could into his short stay. Later, as I became a regular visitor, I soon learnt how and where to avoid the crowds and enjoy the cities' culture rather than their vices. If I had to choose between the two cities, Alex would win every time. I found Cairo to be too rough; it was a bit like a Wild West frontier town, with gambling, saloon bars, and scantily-clad dancing girls jiggling about. Although Cairo could be sophisticated, smart and chic in places, I much preferred the slower pace and cool sea breeze of Alexandria.

The following evening, I was sat on the terrace of the TOC-H with a beer in my hand when in strolled Earnest, with the biggest grin on his face. He had been granted a five-day pass, loaned a truck from the company depot, and driven all day to come and meet me.

Earnest was three years older than me, born three months before the end of WW1 in August 1918. He enlisted right at the start of the war on the 18th September 1939, and joined the Royal Engineers. His outfit was the 290th Army Troops Company Royal Engineers, where he remained throughout the war. His unit was attached to an infantry division and provided a pool of trained engineers or sappers to undertake any engineering task that they needed. They were a self-contained engineer unit with tradesmen of all kinds using specialist machinery. Earnest was a mechanic, or fitter, and his job, he said was "To keep the whole show on the road."

He had been through some tough times; he was even evacuated from Dunkirk with the British Expeditionary Force in 1940. Shortly afterwards, in 1941 he was sent to the Middle East where he had been ever since. He was a Desert Rat through and through — and no stranger to Cairo.

We drank well into the night and I woke the following morning with the worst hangover I had ever had. We had agreed the previous evening that we would visit the pyramids, so in the late afternoon, when we were feeling a little better and when it was much cooler, we set off. It took us just short of an hour to make our way there.

Over the English bridge, the busy city soon gave way to mud brick villages, canals and fields. Farmers were beginning to harvest their crops of beans and barley and wheat before the floods arrived in a few months' time.

We travelled on through mango groves until we reached the Sphinx, which was not looking at its best, and the pyramids, which resembled three giant sentinels guarding the desert. They were monumental, and it was hard to believe that they had been built by primitive people over 3000 years ago. They covered a vast area roughly the size of the farm I worked back home; they had once been alongside the Nile, but the river had slowly changed its route over the centuries and now flowed six miles to the east.

I had heard so many different stories about them, why they were built, and treasures that still lay hidden inside them. They were a a riddle, wrapped in a mystery, inside an enigma, but above all they were simply amazing. If you looked carefully you could just make out that they were once different colours; the great pyramid would have been white, and the others black and red. The great pyramid was made from over two million stones, all stacked up on top of each other.

We did the obligatory ride on the camels and then decided to go inside the Great Pyramid to cool off. We chose a rather wizened frail-looking man as our guide, mainly because he spoke some English and given his age we assumed he was the most knowledgeable there.

He led us up some rather steep stone blocks to a small opening which turned out to be the entrance to the pyramid. The electric lighting was not working, so he gave us candles which we could use to see our way. The place was full of visiting soldiers, and despite only being lit by candlelight, there were so many it was easy to see where you were going. Typically, the whole place smelt like a lavatory, and the stale air was very unpleasant. Occasionally, our guide would light a magnesium flare to illuminate a chamber or an artefact of interest. Soon we reached the central sarcophogus, which was in the middle of the pyramid — a huge place, with massive polished stone slabs all around.

We then did something completely stupid; we paid a small additional fee to be taken into the *secret* chambers above the Grand Gallery. First we had to climb some old rickety wooden ladders and squeeze through a tight hole and fight our way past some Australians to get into a small chamber that looked like a roof loft — but made of stone. I am not normally claustrophbic, but while I was in there I suddenly had a very nervous feeling and wanted to get out; I remember thinking that, despite it having been standing for over 3,000 years, that day could have been the day it decided to collapse in on us.

There were more secret chambers, but we had explored enough and were very pleased when we got out and back into the sun again. Then, because we could, we decided to climb the pyramid. It took about fifteen minutes to get to the top, where we carved our initials alongside Napoleonic troops who had done almost the same 150 years before.

By 6 p.m. the sun was starting to go down, and although it made complete sense to get down whilst we could still see, we decided to stay and watch Cairo twinkle into life. We were blessed with a clear night sky, and although I had marvelled at its beauty so many times, that evening it was something else. The star constellation of Orion was visible to the right of the Milky Way, and we had been told that the layout of the pyramids followed the pattern of the three brightest stars that make up Orion's Belt — Alnitak, Alnilam and Mintaka.

We were back in Cairo a few hours later. Following a quick wash and change, we were out on the town. We managed to blag our way into the restaurant on the roof of the Continental Hotel. It was a popular place, with a dance floor, a cabaret with belly dancers, acrobats and a magician. It was hosted by a beautiful blonde American lady, who wore a long figure-hugging chiffon dress and rounded off the evening show with a solo song and dance routine. Many years later, Earnest and I would often recall that day, the pyramids, and that girl.

We also talked about Ernest's best friend William 'Bill' Hinkley. Earnest had moved into 3 Sun Street, Quarry Bank with our other brother Walter a year prior to joining up. He had become best friends with Bill and his wife Gladys. They had married in 1939 and he had just heard that Gladys had given birth to a girl who they had named Patricia. He joked about how they were trying to "Fix me up with one of Gladys' friends."

On the 29th June, 1944 Corporal 5572974 William Arthur Hingley, aged 26, was killed in Normandy, France D-Day +23 serving with the Fifth Battalion, Wiltshire Regiment. He is buried in the Tilly-Sur-Seulles War Cemetery and his name is engraved on the Quarry Bank War Memorial.

After the war Earnest settled back in Quarry Bank and became a mechanic. He married Gladys on the 10th February 1947 and they had two children together, Shirley and Susan. He died on the 13th February 2011. One of his favourite sayings was, "Whoever said the pen is mightier than the sword obviously never encountered automatic weapons."

24

Oriental Glitter & Magical Perversions

I remember Cairo as a city of extremes, with colourfully-dressed wealthy residents living alongside thousands of homeless beggars who got everywhere and constantly hassled you for money. It was the first time I had seen anyone with leprosy; there was a special hospital just south of our headquarters in Garden City, and lepers were a regular sight.

Officers and men were segregated, with hotels and bars classed as out-of-bounds to other ranks, although later, as a dispatch rider, I had official access to everywhere. British troops were used to segregation, but it was a new concept to the Australians, New Zealanders and South Africans. Some were rich landowners, who had enlisted as private soldiers just to get into the fight early. When the American soldiers and airmen arrived, the *Yankee-Doodle-Dandies*, as we called them, forced a relaxation of the rules.

I had never experienced anything or anywhere like Cairo; you could smell the city long before you would arrive. Its lifeline was the Nile; it was also an open sewer and cases of typhoid were not uncommon. Once in the city, it was an assault on all my senses, bombarding my eyes with bright lights and colours, filling my ears with noise, and exposing my taste buds to spices I had never tasted before — or since. The city aromas that I remember most were the smell of damp apartments, Egyptian tobacco and hashish, the smell of kebabs roasting, and corn cooking on charcoal fires in the early-morning. But most of all the scent of expensive Paris perfume would stop me in my tracks. My nose had been starved for such a long time of anything other than the stench of cordite, oily fumes from burning vehicles, and death.

It was a very noisy, crowded city, with trams clattering, their conductors blowing hunting horns, people shouting, laughing and loving all at the top of their voices.

My favourite pastime was sitting outside a bar at a pavement table drinking coffee and watching the world go by. I would stare at the neon signs and listen to the sound of domino pieces clattering and the gurgling of hash bongs or water pipes in the background. There were soldiers from all the allied armies and uniforms of all kinds. Everyone looked as 'smart as paint', but what stood out most was their different head-dresses. There was the diamond-shaped Polish hat, *Czapkas*, the South African *Solar Topees*, the Indian *Pugrees*, which varied according to the wearer's tribe and religion, and the French K*epis*. The Australians, with their 'wide-awake' hats, pined up on the left whenever they stepped out. The New Zealand hat was similar to the Australian hat, but with a conical crown. Then there were the Greeks, with their olive-green caps with pale blue and white cockades. We were less glamorous, and wore peak caps, except for the tank crews, who wore berets.

On one occasion, the Chief Field Security Officer in Cairo, Major Sansom, dressed two of his men in German uniforms and had them wander around the city to see how vigilant the troops were and to test security. After two days of never being challenged once, the major abandoned the exercise.

The aim of 'first-timers' with only a few days' leave and plenty of back pay was to seek out the dingiest places for drinking, eating, gambling, cabaret and sex. A typical scene would be British soldiers outside a restaurant where English cooking was advertised, with names like *Cafe-Bar Old England*, and *Home Sweet Home*, stuffing themselves with water buffalo steak, eggs and chips, whilst throwing verbal insults at anyone passing by.

Although there were free transit camps available, we chose the TOC-H or other city hotels to stay in, rather than mingling with the transit troops. We would often take a room together; although we never used the room except to sleep off our drunken excesses. Any free floor space was taken-up with crates of beer, whiskey and any other contraband we could get our hands on.

There was the obligatory visit to the local Woolworths to stock up on medical supplies, ointments and creams to aid desert sores.

Drinking could be a hazardous experience, not just because of the poor quality of the alcohol, but because there was a shortage of beer glasses. The locals converted empty beer bottles by removing the tops and turning the bodies into makeshift glasses; it wasn't uncommon to cut your lip or hand on them.

A traditional Cairo ritual was to drink the deadly Egyptian *Zebeeb*. It was made from raisins, infused with ginger and whisky. It came as a small shot, and you either poured it into a glass of cold water or straight into your beer to make a lethal Ginger Beer cocktail.

Not surprisingly, with all the drinking and young men often fresh out of combat, there were many bar room brawls. Fights would often break out due to a belief that we were being fleeced by the locals or because some poor RAF chap had passed by and been blamed for the absence of aircraft over the battlefield. They were mostly over as quickly as they started, and long before the Military Police would arrive. Heavy drinking and the occasional bar fight were generally accepted; street violence was a different matter, and would result in a heavy police response, with swift military justice from boots and batons. Sadly for the bar-owners, there was no compensation for any damage that occurred; it was seen as an occupational hazard.

The first few days were often a blur of excess. Lunch was at Groppi's, located close to Shepheard's Hotel; it was very expensive, but the grub was great and was one of the few posh places that we were allowed into. I was told that it modelled itself on the Ritz in London; having never been, I wouldn't know. In the evenings I drank at the popular Blue Nile Cabaret; it was here that we would sit for hours with the *Cherry Brandy Girls*. The Blue Nile was just a drinking bar; prostitution was banned, and there were lots of attractive girls who would happily sit and listen to our war stories and tell us how brave we were — that was as long as you kept buying them the overpriced shots of cherry brandy. That did not matter, as I enjoyed the company, and they smelt great and looked beautiful. There was also the Kit Kat Club, which was a boat moored on the Nile; it was very nice, but we were told it was full of spies and that we should be careful what we said when talking to the Hungarian dancing girls. Then there was the Bosphore Club; it was a bit too close to the Military Police Headquarters in Bad-el-Hadid for my liking, but it was convenient for the trams and you would be pretty safe from trouble before moving on to the clubs and cabarets around Sharia Emad Ed Din.

But soon the money started to run-out. I said goodbye to the posh living and cherry brandy girls, and having got the need out of my system, settled down to enjoy my leave quietly.

"Egypt was known as the land of the three Ss:
Sun, Sand and Syphilis."

In Alex, the brothels were on Sister Street, and in Cairo prostitution concentrated itself around the main streets in the centre of the town. The most popular location was Shari el-Berka, an area of ill-repute better known as *The . Berka*. The Berka was for rank and file troops. Just opposite was the fashionable Shepherd's Hotel, which was off-limits to other ranks and was the place where officers met their lady friends. It was said that "You would get a dose just by smelling the air in the Berka!" The prostitutes would sit on little balconies fanning themselves and calling down to the soldiers below, whilst their pimps would proposition you on the street. They would stop you and say, "You want my sister, very nice, very clean, all pink inside like Queen Victoria," and queues would form for the best girls.

One famous Berka prostitute was known as *Tiger Lil*, and she would proudly boast that she had served all our fathers during the First World War, and she was prepared to school us in the art of sex too. There were also peep shows and pornographic cabarets; the most famous of these was in Darling Street, which featured two fat women and a donkey.

The Berka had actually been closed for a short period in 1942, after it was reported that some Australians had been throwing prostitutes out of windows. Now more men ended up in hospital with venereal disease than were wounded by the enemy. Treatment meant soldiers were taken from their units for three weeks or more at a time.

It was impossible to ban soldiers from having sex, so the authorities tried to control and prevent the spread of the disease. The army's solution was to inform and educate the troops with information on the dangers of the disease and, when that failed, soldiers would be put on a charge, resulting in a loss of pay.

There were powerful groups of 'do-gooders' back in Britain; they campaigned tirelessly to prevent men having access to sex. By 1943, the local authorities had enforced controls within the red-light districts; some of the worst brothels had been closed down, and some areas classed as out-of-bounds. Prostitutes underwent regular medical checks, and the army even set-up a stall in the Berka with a medical officer who handed out French Letters, ointment and advice. I thought the best way to educate soldiers was a visit to Cairo's Hygiene Museum, where there was a remarkable collection of plaster casts of male sexual organs, in every stage of gonorrhoea and syphilis.

I did venture into the Berka, mainly out of curiosity, but also because if you didn't you were branded as lacking in some way! I have to say that the place was absolutely filthy, and I couldn't imagine any place less likely to arouse my passion, no matter how drunk I got. I also considered my health to be important, and did not want to chance my luck. Besides, I fancied my chances with the uniformed girls that were present in the city. This was because there was a great demand for clerical staff and there were plenty of willing volunteers from the South African, Women's Auxiliary Army Service (Wasses) and British, Auxiliary Territorial Service (ATS).

I enjoyed visiting the sights and museums; they offered an intriguing mixture of old and new, east meets west, civilian and military. During the day, I would jump on one of the clanging trams and travel to a different part of the city, which was much too large to walk across. I would watch in amazement as the conductors, swinging along the outside of the trams, would collect fares without falling off. At the same time, I was also very cautious of pick-pockets, who were experts at their craft.

One activity that was very popular among rival soldiers was the practice of *gharries racing*. This would involve commandeering a horse-drawn taxi or gharry, replacing the horses with soldiers and racing between different bars, frightening the locals, but to cheers of encouragement from spectators. Rivalries between the RAF and the army would draw large crowds and extensive betting on the outcome of the race. On many occasions, taxi drivers refused to allow solders in their cabs because all too often they didn't pay and just ran off. But the military propaganda machine worked its magic; you often saw pictures of laughing soldiers and gharry-boys posing together in the papers.

Another popular and safer pastime was going to the cinemas. There were several scattered around the city, and even an open air one in Ezbekieh Gardens, which was next to Shepherd's Hotel. The audience would comprise mostly soldiers and a few educated Egyptians, dressed in European suits and wearing red fezzes. At the end of every performance, they always played the Egyptian national anthem, and we would disrespectfully sing along with a rude song.

"King Farouk, King Farouk you dirty old crook.
As you walk down the street in your 50 shilling suit.
Queen Farida's very gay, cos she's in the family way."

25
Christmas 1943

On the 1st December 1943, along with the others from off the DR course, I reported for duty at Mustapha Barracks, our headquarters in Alexandria. We were given new motorbikes and our assignments. They split us up by posting us to different areas of the command, where we were to spend a three-month stint after which we would be rotated.

This was the second time I had volunteered for different duties, the first being on the radar and now dispatch riding. They say never volunteer for anything, but it was working out well for me, so far. It didn't take too long to adjust to this more civilised way of life after my nomadic war-weary existence in the desert.

I started my first stint in Alexandria; my area of responsibility was HQ Eighteenth AA Brigade, with the Twenty-seventh, 131st and 121st LAA Regiments in the Mustapha area. The 104th AA Defence HQ was protecting the harbour at Ras-el-Tin, and the 149th LAA Battery was high on the hillside at Rue Corniche, in Kom-el-Dik; it was a dangerous location to reach, especially when it was raining.

I assumed a dual role; whilst I mostly delivered messages, I was also an officer driver (OD), which was the formal description for officer's 'taxi'. I would often take officers on the back of my bike to wherever they needed to go. Bikes, whilst not as comfortable as staff cars, were a lot faster, especially when trying to navigate through busy towns and cities. Carrying dispatches and sometimes passengers meant knowing exactly where to go and how to get there; not just the quickest routes but those to avoid, as such treacherous routes could lead to the enemy, minefields or worse, hostile locals!

Dispatches marked 'secret' were easy to deliver, as they could be left with the duty clerk. However, those marked 'top secret' had to be handed over to the named officer it was addressed to. This had its perks, as often it would involve searching around military buildings, hotels, officer's clubs and bars, which would have normally been out-of-bounds to me. I never had any knowledge of the contents of any messages, but looking at the expression on the faces of the recipients, I would guess most were shopping lists of essentials they needed to bring back to camp. It was very rare to pass on a verbal message; when I did they were mostly along the lines of, "You're needed back at HQ immediately." They would jump on the back of the bike and we would weave our way to the destination.

One regular and important route was back and forth between the different hospitals and headquarters, to let the medics know how many wounded soldiers to expect coming back from Italy. We also informed HQ of how many were being discharged and could be sent back to the front line.

DR life was always busy, and sometimes dangerous, but for me it was heaven. We were told, "Not to take unnecessary risks," and then they would tell us, "To deliver the messages in the fastest possible time."

It was not unusual to cover over 200 miles in a day, regardless of the weather conditions. Riding in the winter was the worst, especially as the mud would stick to the tyres and eventually jam itself against the mud guards. It got so bad that I would have to remove the guards, which resulted in mud flying everywhere. I lost count of the amount of times I needed to get off the road quickly to avoid being hit by a tank or truck, which along with the weather posed the biggest danger to us. Fatigue and accidents were the new enemy, and more riders were killed this way than were killed in combat.

I still had my Thompson sub machine-gun, but I stopped slinging it over my back after I fell off my bike, landed on it, and injured myself. I was also issued with a Webley 45; it was a nice pistol, but I never got to fire it at anybody; I just used it for target practice on lizards. I also had a German Luger pistol, which I had traded for a box of Macedonian cigars and a few bottles of Brandy. It was a poor trade; I soon discovered why the previous owner was so willing to exchange. After several shots, the pistol would jam. I eventually got a German prisoner to show me how to strip and clean it, and he told me that, if I got the chance, I should exchange it for an earlier version, as they were much more reliable.

I remember hearing countless stories from our troops who had been released from captivity having been taken prisoner earlier in the campaign. Everyone said, how well they had been treated by the Germans. That was not said about the treatment at the hands of their Italian captors. The German POWs knew this, and would keep their distance from their former allies.

My new duties started during a period of intense activity, with the whole brigade going through a rigorous training programme. Headquarters tried their best to adjust my daily routine to ensure I could participate, and I did my best to avoid it. When they did catch up with me, it was the same old physical training, bayonet fighting, and climbing up and down rope ladders. They had us swimming in full kit with all our spare clothing wrapped inside our gas capes. The idea was that the bundle would act as a buoyancy aid whilst keeping our kit dry. It worked to a degree, but failed more often than not. It wasn't all combat training; they still had us marching around the parade square in an attempt to improve discipline. I do remember learning two new skills; how to get my bike up a cliff using ropes and winches, and how to fire my Thompson machine-gun whilst riding my bike.

To ensure everyone received the training, the brigade needed to rotate its units between No.1 AA Practice Camp at El Deir, the 158th Transit Camp at Amiriya, and the operational sites around Abouker, Amiriya, Heliopolis and Qassassin. I and other riders were tasked with marking out convoy routes and guiding troops and vehicles when they were on the move. I spent days making sign posts out of the metal from petrol cans, symbols like a bottle, a boat and a hat.

I can only remember my first 'shuffle' of many. I guided the Twenty-seventh LAA a short distance to the RAF airfield at Amiriya. I then travelled down to Cairo where I collected a small convoy from the Twenty-third HAA, who had come up from El Deir Training camp to replace the 683rd HAA Abouker. Most of the regiment had travelled by train, but they had been tasked with bringing spare guns up to Alex for onward sea passage. I brought them the final leg to the east of Alexandria.

One day just before Christmas, I was sent to Cairo to deliver a dispatch to the British Ninth General Hospital. The hospital was in the process of moving back to England, but had been used since September 1941 as a burns unit. Despite there being no patients left, the place still stank of burnt flesh; it was horrible, and it brought back terrible memories. Most of those I was now with had not experienced even a small fraction of the 'excitement' I had seen from Gazala to Alamein, and beyond. It was difficult to explain, or for people to understand; only those who had been on the journey knew. For that reason, we veterans stuck together and kept our distance from others.

"The futility of war had been adequately demonstrated to me."

Christmas soon arrived; I had lunch in the barracks served by our officers, and then in the evening I went dancing with nurses at the WMCA. Before the meal, I went down to the beach to watch a football match that had been arranged between the army and navy. The navy team comprised mostly Royal Marines from No.1 and No.42 Commandos on their way to Bangkok, and the army team was made up of off-duty Royal Artillery soldiers. It was great fun; the referee arrived mounted on a camel, and trotted around the beach blowing his whistle to roars of laughter. The game was going our way when someone threw a smoke grenade onto the pitch and the match had to end, 'due to fog'. A draw was announced, and we all headed back to the bar for lunch. It was a memorable Christmas, and a more civilised affair than in previous years. I had soup, followed by turkey with all the trimmings, Christmas pudding with white sauce, and a mince pie, all washed down with beer.

It was all going well until I was taken aside by a sergeant who wanted to discuss my uniform and some *recommendations* he had in mind. I was wearing an Indian army shirt, non-issue corduroy trousers, and sand shoes, as well as an Italian high-neck jumper which had once been the property of our enemy. The only bit of original kit that I was wearing was my hat. He had a point; the Eighth Army (the Desert Rats) had its own dress-code, 'the Eighth Army style', which had been tolerated whilst Montgomery was in charge. But we were now in a different army, and although his point was well-made, it was not well-received on my part.

26
The Eighth Army Manner

There was a close brotherhood amongst those of us who had been part of the Middle East Force (MEF); we called ourselves "the Men England Forgot." The bond was especially close for those of us who had fought at Gazala and El Alamein; we had earned the title of Desert Rats, for we were the ones that had turned the tide of the war by beating Rommel, and his *Deutsches Afrikakorps*.

The Eighth Army had been isolated from other armies, and as a result we developed our own culture in the way we dressed, spoke and behaved. The shortage of equipment and supplies, combined with the harsh desert conditions, meant that we adapted our equipment, and especially our uniforms, to suit the environment and to make them as bearable as possible. Looking back, it also had a lot to do with the pan-imperial and diverse mixture of the Eighth Army soldiers that I served alongside; Australians, New Zealanders, South Africans, Indians, Free French and Polish soldiers, who all brought their mannerisms into the melting-pot that was the Eighth Army.

The last thing on our minds was to look smart or conform to any military dress code. The first thing I changed was my standard-issue tropical baggy shorts, which were useless. They were actually very uncomfortable baggy trousers that rolled-up to make stupid looking shorts that we called 'shit-stoppers.' I cut them off above the knee to make pants and to let the sun get to my lily-white legs. I also got rid of my issue ammo boots for 'desert boots', made of soft canvas with a thick sole to resist thorns which we called 'brothel creepers.' For most of the time I existed in a dishevelled state, in my bleached khaki shorts and shirt, with a handkerchief tied around the face covering the nose and mouth in an attempt to keep the dust at bay, like a cowboy. I would practically never wear a helmet until it was too dangerous to go without. Having never been issued with sunglasses, because of the glare from the sun and the need to be constantly on the lookout for enemy planes, I had a permanent squint. Added to this, a piece of cotton, covered with Vaseline and placed into the ear was the only protection I had from the noise of the guns; this meant I was partially deaf. The desert had made its mark on my body; my skin was a brick-red colour, and my arms and legs were covered in scars from desert sores.

I had a casual and bloody-minded manner about me; I was hostile towards the new arrivals from England who had "not got their knees brown." I knew it was no fault of theirs. The only way that they could join the club would be to prove themselves in battle, but the war had moved on, and there was little chance or opportunity for them to do so. Officers had always been able to adapt their uniforms, and it was not long before they were dressed in the most non-regulation uniforms you could imagine. They were often very flashy, with brightly-coloured cravats and carrying fly whisks, which made them stand out from the crowd; I have to say, I loved to see it. Once the officers started it, it became a free-for-all and new arrivals did whatever they could to fit in with the rest of us by altering and even trying to age their uniforms.

Our officers' bizarre mixture of military and non-military clothes and flamboyant dress inspired an artist called John

Jones to create a cartoon called *The Two Types*. Jon, as he became known, was commissioned into the army in 1938, and served in the Welsh Regiment in North Africa. Whilst convalescing from shell-shock, he started drawing cartoons of a pair of battle-hardened British Officers — Captains Fortescue and Ffoulks. He sent his cartoons to the British Army Newspaper Unit. They were accepted and made their first appearance in the Eighth Army News in July 1944, under the title *Two Smile*, which later, in August, changed to *The Two Types*. The cartoons were very popular with the troops, but not with everyone; Montgomery banned one cartoon which showed them in a trench at El Alamein with German tanks approaching, accompanied by the caption "When this lot's over, I bet some ruddy general proposes a reunion!" Despite complaining about the cartoon, Montgomery got in on the act himself and traded his staff officer's peaked cap for a black beret and an Australian bush hat which he covered in the different cap badges of units in his command.

However, the maintenance of high standards in acceptable dress was required at some of the high-end clubs in the cities. There was a story going around that Noel Coward, who was a very famous actor and known for his sense of personal style, was even thrown out of the Royal Yacht Club in Alexandria for wearing shorts and a shirt!

For those of us who were still in the Mediterranean in July 1944, when the D-Day landings took place, our past successes were forgotten when Lady Astor called the men of the Eighth Army 'D-Day Dodgers'. Lady Astor was already an unpopular person because of her moral campaign against drink and prostitution over previous years. She was also not very popular with Winston Churchill; on one occasion, she commented that he was drunk, to which he responded, "You are ugly, but at least I will be sober in the morning!" During another encounter, she said to him, "If you were my husband, I would give you poison." He is said to have replied, "If I were your husband, I would drink it."

So, whilst Captains Fortescue and Ffoulks left North Africa and continued their cartoon journey with the Eighth Army in Italy, I remained behind to face an establishment looking to bring the veterans back into a more conventional manner of behaviour and dress. They introduced a strict dress code; badges and chevrons all had to be in the right place; even our ties had to be the right shade. We couldn't wear anklets, which are small khaki web gaiters that were perfect at keeping debris from getting inside your boots. We did try to make our mark by having our pullovers visible below our battle dress blouses, buttoning them to the top and wearing tie pins, but they soon put a stop to it. It would be fair to say that I resisted with every ounce of effort I could muster. Being on the bikes was a blessing because it kept me clear of the regiment, and we wore overalls which hid what I wore underneath, which was often banned.

I would never be alone for long when out drinking in Alexandria or Cairo; anyone who had served as a Desert Rat was a brother-in-arms; we flocked together, drinking, laughing and fighting alongside one another. I will always remember those days with immense pride.

27
Bitten By The Elephant

January 1944 was colder than previous years, but a lot quieter and safer. I was now billeted in the heart of Alexandria at the Brigade Headquarters; but despite being in a building, the nights were still very cold. I would sleep in my stiff, smelly socks, with my shirt tucked into my long underwear and a stocking cap on my head. I would wriggle my way into my sleeping bag under a pile of blankets and sleep until woken for stand-to or to undertake dispatch rider duties.

At the beginning of January, I had to drive our Intelligence Officer, Captain Loynes, to Cairo to attend a course because he had missed the morning train. I remember, because I drove him down in one of the newly-issued American Jeeps. It was a pleasure to drive; very responsive, very fast, and it had less than 100 miles on the clock. It also meant I was able to keep my head down for a few days, whilst a Chinese Military Mission inspected the Anti-Aircraft defences around Alexandria. It was all spit, polish and smiley faces, and I was better off away from it. I stopped in Cairo overnight with the intention of having a few drinks with the lads before heading back the next day. Instead, I spent all night worrying that someone would steal the jeep. Thankfully, it was still parked in the GHQ compound the next morning, and I took a slow drive back to Alex, returning just in time for the evening meal.

Shortly afterwards, I received orders to assist guiding the 191st and 648th HAA Regiments from Alexandria to the Number Two Practice Camp in Nahariya, Palestine, a journey that would take two long days. We set-off early in the morning, with everyone shouting at each other and whistling dance tunes as we left; that was something we always seemed to do. From Alexandria, we headed for Port Said where we crossed the Suez Canal and into the Sinai Desert. We travelled close to the sea until we reached the salt flats where we headed inland before stopping for the night. The next day, we crossed into Palestine and followed the coastal road to Gaza; we went through the towns of Al-Ramala, Jaffa with its orange trees everywhere, Tulkarm, Hadera, and Haifa, before finally reaching our destination by the sea at Nahariya, twenty miles north of the city of Haifa.

Hadera, became a favourite rest-stop of mine over that period; I would stop in the village whenever I passed through. It was like an oasis located on the Sharon plain, between the dunes of the Mediterranean and the Judean hills. It had two main streets carrying traffic travelling between Tel Aviv and Haifa, and was a popular stopping point for passing service vehicles. It had plenty of cafes, signs everywhere advertising 'real English food', 'egg and chips', 'beer' and 'Gazouz Tea', which was a Tunisian mint tea and very refreshing. My favourite was a café called *Soldiers Home*, and the host was a Jewish lady who came from Liverpool. Other cafes had Jewish owners displaced by the war from all over Europe. Hadera was pleasant enough during the winter, but in the summer the outsides of the buildings would become black with flies. It was also a very busy place, with buses, camels, cars and military vehicles constantly on the move. There were Arabs wearing their striped nightshirts and white keffiyeh, while the Jewish girls all wore blue bloomers and white blouses, like a uniform.

The next day, we raced back to Alex on our bikes and a few days later repeated the trip, shepherding the 118th and 648th HAA Regiments along the same route. By now I was becoming familiar with the route, and wanted to explore the area further. It didn't take me too long to convince the other DRs that an alternative return route would make a change, and we agreed to go back via Jerusalem and the Dead Sea for a bit of sightseeing. First, we headed through Jerusalem and then six miles south and up into the mountains to reach Bethlehem. Once we arrived, we visited The Church of the Nativity in the centre of the city, which is built over a cave called the Holy Crypt, where Jesus was supposedly born. We were disappointed and just stood around looking at each other. I guess after all the Sunday School lessons I was expecting to see a stable with a manger in the corner!

We stopped for a drink at the Jacir Palace, close to the church, before moving on. We were hounded by beggars shouting *"Howajji, bucksheesh! howajji, bucksheesh! howajji, bucksheesh! bucksheesh! bucksheesh!"* "Baksheesh" is a Persian word which, roughly translated, means 'tip', or sometimes a bribe. The word was soon introduced into our everyday slang as 'Buckshee', and referred to any kit or equipment that could be offered as a gift or was 'off the record' or 'going spare'.

We left the beggars in a cloud of dust, headed back through Jerusalem and then west towards Kalya, which was located on the northwest bank of the Dead Sea. The route to Kalya was challenging; in under an hour you drop from three thousand feet above sea level to more than 1,500 feet below. The pressure on the eardrums in the Jordan Valley is indescribable, making your ears go deaf and painful. This was a strange and unsettling experience when you didn't know what was happening to you. The winding road, with its sharp bends and precipices, was fun to travel down, but mentally and physically exhausting. We passed Jericho on our left, with its banana groves, and then encountered a white sign telling us we were at Sea Level, before descending another mile into the Jordan valley. The patches of grass and flocks of sheep soon gave way to a desolate land on which there were no living creatures, no grass no bushes, no birds — nothing!

We stopped by the side of the Dead Sea at the only cafe in the area; we stripped-off and plunged into the water, but not for long. It felt horrible and slimy; it was like having a very salty bath and it was impossible to sink. We left and raced along the west bank of the Dead Sea before heading back to the coast where we had a quick swim in the Mediterranean to clean up before we were on our way again.

Crossing the Sinai, we came across a small collection of Jeeps with the occupants dressed in the familiar ragtag style of the Eighth Army. They turned out to be members of the Long Range Desert Group who were in the area training. We stopped and had a chat and laughed about all our shenanigans in Cairo over a cuppa char which they made for us. They told us about the best places to go in Beirut, which were the Salvation Army Hostel and the famous Kit Kat Club. We agreed that if we were to see each other again at the Kit Kat, we would drink the place dry. They then scrounged a few cigars and a bottle of orange gin before we went our separate ways. The Long Range Desert Group, who we jokingly called the Short Range, Shepherds' Group, went on to become the Special Air Service.

The newspapers were full of the news that the Battle for Monte Casino had started in Italy and there had been a huge British air raid on Berlin. It felt like the war would soon be over.

At the end of the month, an enemy JU88 was flying a reconnaissance mission over Alexandria. It was spotted too late, and the batteries were only able to fire eleven rounds and failed to hit it. All hell broke loose with accusations that the Anti-Aircraft troops were starting to *switch-off*.

In mid-February I escorted the Thirteenth and Fifty-fourth HAA from Tabruk to Sidi Bishr, Alexandria. In preparation, I spent a few days in Tabruk which, despite still being heavily damaged, was trying its best to return to normality. The Italians had occupied Libya in 1912, and by the outbreak of war in 1939, the Italians represented around about 25% of the population of the city. They had also built the main coastal road and the railway, which we were now using to get around, as well as having a considerable influence on the architecture and culture of the city. In comparison, Alexandria had been populated by the Greeks; a favourite snack of mine was Greek flat bread with cheese called plakountos. In Tabruk, you could get something similar, but they called them piazza.

By March the weather was starting to warm up, and with it malaria became widespread. This was because the mosquito population had increased dramatically due to untreated stagnant ponds along the Suez and Nile waterways. Thankfully, I was able to acquire a mosquito net which I kept with me at all times.

One evening I was turfed out of my bed just before midnight and sent to Alexandria marina to taxi an officer who was to arrive by motor launch down to Cairo. After a long wait, my passenger arrived wearing filthy battledress and sporting a huge black beard. I soon discovered that he was with the Special Operations Executive (SOE). He never said where he had been, but I guessed it was probably with the partisans in Greece, Albania or Yugoslavia. I dropped him off at a block of flats called the Rustum Building, not far from the General Headquarters, which was where SOE Cairo was based.

Towards the end of the month I received orders that I was going to be rotated and I would join Second HAA's Regimental Headquarters in Tabruk at the end of April. I was ready for a move; the headquarters in Alex had become the holding location for troops fresh out of hospital and who were not fit or able to join operational units. They brought too much attention to themselves and got in the way. There were lads who were trying to work their ticket by pretending they were mad by refusing 'to soldier' and not wearing uniform or carrying out orders. There were also recovering alcoholics and drug users.

I liked my drink, especially a drop of whisky, gin or brandy, but it was always in moderation, except during the odd celebration. Besides, we were rationed with only a quarter of a bottle per person each month. You could get smuggled booze which came in from Cyprus or fake Palestinian gins and whisky which made you ill. I never touched drugs, but many did.

"How do you survive when it is raining fire and death?"
"You drink a cuppa Soma."

For those who chose that route and became addicted, there was a phrase we used; we would say, "They had been bitten by the elephant." Medics would hand out 'alertness aids' like sweets. The most common was an inhaler called Benzedrine, which contained a drug called amphetamine that would make you more alert. We called them "bennies", and troops would break the container open, remove a paper strip from inside, which was covered in Benzedrine, tear it into small pieces, roll them into small balls, and swallow them. Pilots were given bennies and Methedrine, nicknamed 'go-pills' to keep them awake and alert during long missions. The RAF boys used to joke that without go-pills they would never have won the Battle of Britain.

A lot of German prisoners suffered withdrawal symptoms when in captivity because they had been given a pill called Pervitin. We were even told to keep clear of German-issued chocolate, as it was rumoured to be laced with chemicals. Most of the armies were giving drugs to their troops; the Soviet one was called Vint or Screw, and the Japanese gave their soldiers Shabu. We even supplied Benzedrine to the Americans; I once read that the allies used over 150 million amphetamine tablets during the war.

It was easy to get hold of other drugs if you wanted. There was the local herbal drug called Khat, or Qat, which could be chewed or made into tea-pads and brewed in hot water to make a cuppa Soma. There was also hashish or cannabis, barbiturates and opium available openly in the bazaars. This was in addition to the medical stocks captured from the enemy or recovered from downed aircraft and from shipwrecks around the harbours, which were being sold on the black market.

During the war, a lot of drugs that are now illegal were still legal. Cocaine was not even seen as dangerous or addictive at all. You could go to any chemist in Cairo or Alexandria and buy Benzedrine over the counter without a doctor's note. In those days, there was hospital treatment for the three Rs — responsibility, rehabilitation and resettlement, but it was aimed at those with physical injuries. They were just starting to take mental trauma seriously, but for self-inflicted injuries like alcoholism and drug addiction, treatment was pretty crude. Mainly sufferers were given hospital isolation for a period of time to *get clean*, and then sent back to their units, who would look for the medical officers to declare them fit to soldier.

28
Operation Picnic - 'Mutiny'

There were now more friendly aircraft flying overhead than there were enemy aircraft, and the spotters were being over-cautious. Because of this, when an enemy aircraft was eventually identified, it would be too late, and almost impossible to hit the plane. Because of this, the officers came up with a new operating procedure and we were given fresh instructions on what to do when an approaching aircraft was spotted and could possibly be hostile. First, all the guns would be placed on stand-to, then, on receipt of the order "Scram", one of the guns would fire a warning shot set to burst at 6,000 feet. Our pilots knew not to fly at this height, and to make themselves known as friendly when challenged. The word 'scram' was American slang, and meant 'go away'.

The American troops had their own language; they would start sentences with "Say", "Say, chap, you got a smoke?" and if something was wrong or silly it was *applesauce* or *baloney* Despite sharing a common language, more often than not I was unable to understand a word they were saying! They were fascinated by my Black Country accent and would constantly say, "Say Mac, talk to me, say something." If they were going to fight they would say "Put up your dukes"; dukes were fists. They would also say, "I'm going to smack you in the puss," "snooze" or "hooter," which were all words for nose. If they got thrown out of a bar, that was known as a "bum's rush". They also used lots of abbreviations; the one I remember being used the most was "PDQ", meaning pretty damn quickly. "Say bud, deliver this message PDQ."

April 1944 started off routinely enough, and despite better telephone communication, I was as busy as ever. I spent the first week travelling between Alexandria and Tabruk carrying dispatches or directing convoys. The desert remained a very dangerous place; they were still discovering previously unmapped minefields, especially around the Tabruk area, so we never left designated roads and tracks and avoided movement at night through fear of leaving the road by mistake and wandering into a minefield.

On the 7th I was about to escort B Troop Sixteenth Battery from Alex to Tabruk, when the Greeks mutinied.

In 1941, the Germans occupied Greece. The military personnel and escaping refugees who had made their way to Egypt were formed into the first and second Greek Brigades. They also formed the Royal Hellenic Navy and a merchant fleet which was anchored at Alexandria. By 1944, many of the Greeks in Egypt wanted to see a radical change in the way their homeland would be governed once the Germans had been forced out; a group of officers from the Greek army, navy and air force were demanding a government of national unity.

On the 2nd April, a small group of rebels from the Second Brigade came into Cairo from their camp at Mena and took over the office of the Greek Protestant Marshal before barricading themselves inside. This was the start of the mutiny, and shortly afterwards they were joined by troops from the first Greek brigade at Boufg el Arab.

On the 6th, Greek soldiers formed pickets at their camps to prevent any non-sympathisers to the cause from escaping. The mutineers also manned the Bofors Battery, forcing the bewildered onlookers to move back.

By the 8th, the revolt had spread to Alexandria, where hundreds of Greek seamen, armed with knives and rifles, occupied the union's office in Muhammad Ali Square. Five warships from the Royal Hellenic Navy and a number of Greek merchant vessels also joined the mutiny.

I was dispatched to Ninety-first HAA, whose orders were to report to the docks at Alexandria for guard duty. They were already prepared to deploy, and I returned to the docks with one officer, eleven sergeants, and ninety-one soldiers. The operation was named *Picnic*, and the Ninety-first had orders not to let anyone else leave or enter the harbour. By the 11th the first Greek brigade tried to open negotiations; the offer was rejected, and only unconditional surrender was deemed acceptable; the atmosphere became very tense indeed. There was then an uneasy 'stand-off' which lasted for nearly two weeks. We joked about mutinying ourselves at the time because our tobacco rations had gone mouldy whilst in the stores.

*"Ninety-nine percent of war is a yawn,
one percent a nervous twitch."*

"Sometimes a cloud would pass by the moon and its shadows would race across the sand, leaping over bushes and race towards you. The sudden movement if caught in the corner of your eye would make

you reach for the safety catch on your weapon and your heart would miss a beat..."

Everyone was twitchy; on the evening of the 13th, an unidentified craft was spotted about two miles out at sea and close to the harbour. All defences were manned, with orders to "wait" whilst a motor launch was sent to investigate. We were also ordered to lower and 'bed' the barrage balloons because a Wellington Bomber had been sent to investigate. The radar crew announced that they had located the Wellington, only to be told that it had not yet left the airfield! At the same time, reports came in that unknown armoured vehicles had been reported in the area. We were back on a war footing. The motor launch returned with nothing to report; the Wellington never left the airfield, and the vehicles turned out to be friendly. The balloons went back up and we were stood down just after midnight.

The final stage of the mutiny happened on the 23rd April, when a small British force opened fire on the rebel camp at Mena and the first Greek Brigade surrendered. By the evening of the 24th April, all the rebel ships also surrendered after they were boarded by Greek marines.

The timing could not have been better; we were all stood down, which was great news because over the 24th, 25th and 26th April, the Middle Eastern Concert Party was performing in Tabruk, and I had been granted five days' leave, which I took in Cairo.

29

The Holy Lands

In early May, 1944, I returned from leave in Cairo and found myself attached to the Second HAA Regimental Headquarters, based in Tabruk. I was assigned to general dispatch rider duties and they called me a *Gofor,* which was short for 'go for this and go for that'!

The big news everyone was talking about was that British troops were fighting a decisive battle in Burma at Kohima and Imphal, and the Battle of Monte Casino in Italy had just ended. But, of more importance were rumours of treasure aboard sunken ships in Tabruk harbour. The biggest booty of all was said to be east of the old Italian patrol jetty in the wreck of the San Giorgio. However, nearly all of the regiment was in the desert undergoing training at the practice ranges, too far away from Tabruk, and so they had no opportunity to loot the wrecks.

Whenever I delivered dispatches to the practice camp, all they could talk about was getting back to salvage the treasure before anyone else did, and what they would do with their share. As well as the new Heavy Anti-Aircraft guns the Americans had provided, we were also given Anti-Aircraft Light Machine-Guns (AALMG). These were Bren guns mounted on tripods, and I had a go at trying to hit targets that were being towed behind an RAF aircraft. I never hit anything, but it was fun. The regiment also practiced infantry tactics and assault attacks, but I made myself scarce when that training took place.

April and May had been a quiet period for the Ack-Ack guns around Tabruk and Alexandria. The only targets were enemy reconnaissance aircraft which, frustratingly, flew out of the range of our guns. However, this did not stop the gun crews from trying, and the opportunity to relieve the boredom by expending more ammunition and rockets than really necessary was taken — this did not go down well with the top brass, because they never hit any of the targets!

At the beginning of May, our Commanding Officer, Colonel Bayliss, was constantly travelling back and forth to the Twelfth Army Headquarters in Cairo. Rumours that we were going to be sent back home to be mobilised for the invasion of Europe were making everyone excited and nervous in equal measure. As usual, the rumours were wrong, and on the 15th May we received orders to move, not to England, but to Haifa in Palestine, and the regiment returned from practice camp to prepare for the move.

With less than a week left in Tabruk before we had to depart, our minds were more on the treasure than on the task at hand, which was preparing for the move. Unfortunately, we never got the chance. The docks were designated out-of-bounds, mainly due to the rumours of the treasure aboard the ships, as foolhardy attempts to find it had resulted in several deaths. All we could do was sit on the harbour wall, stare out at the wrecks, and dream of what might have been.

What made things worse was the fact that the only beach with clean swimming water was at a place called Anzac Cove. But this beach was designated for officers only, meaning everyone else was restricted to the harbour area. This was not popular, as it was heavily polluted with toilet waste from the city, diesel oil from wrecked ships, and unexploded bombs. To make things even more intolerable, there were warnings that we could catch anthrax from the waste being poured into the sea by the locals curing animal skins.

On the 20th May we permanently withdrew from all six of our artillery sites from Aboukir to Quassassin. Our orders were to move to a staging area in Haifa, Palestine, and deposit our guns and radar stations at the Base Ordnance Depots (BOD) on our way.

With six days' rations each, we set off. We first travelled to Fort Capuzzo, just west of Sollum for an overnight stop, then via Mersa Matruh and onto RAF El Daba, west of Alexandria, on the 22nd. The next day, the regiment moved to Amirya, but I went with E Troop to Abu Mena, where we handed over one of our radar stations before re-joining the regiment at Amirya. The next day we went to Ismailia on the east bank of the Suez Canal, where we handed over twenty 3.7 anti-aircraft guns and five predictor fire control units.

Two days later, after crossing the Sinai desert, we eventually arrived in Tulkarm, Palistine, where we handed over the last of our equipment and made our way to a staging camp near Haifa.

A few days later, we occupied the artillery sites belonging to the Ninety-fourth HAA and the regiment was now in a 'static role'. Our function was to prevent the enemy from maintaining airbases along the Aegean coastline and to protect the oil installation at Haifa.

The month of June was given over to training and familiarisation on an exercise called *Bullseye*. For everyone else, the war continued, and on the 6th June, the allies launched the largest amphibious invasion in history when they landed on the northern coast of France in a place called Normandy — the invasion of Europe had started.

I did not like Palestine; it had a strange uneasy feel about it. The war had brought about a period of relative peace between the Arab and Jewish populations. Now that the war was starting to look like it could end soon, tensions started to rise, and the British army was not popular — for good reason. I learnt that the modern history of British involvement in Palestine started during WW1. Before the war, Christians, Arabs and Jews all lived in reasonable harmony. The region was also known as the Holy Lands, with Jerusalem being its capital city. The three regional religions, Christianity, Judaism and Islam, all considered it to be their Holy City. In 1914, we were at war with Germany, Austria, Hungary and the Ottoman Empire. Palestine was part of a huge area of the Middle East ruled by the Ottoman Turkish Empire, where the occupants, regardless of religion, were all called Palestinians.

By 1916, Britain was losing the war; German U-boats had starved Britain of the food and the military supplies it needed to continue waging war, and the country was close to starvation. At the same time, the French army had mutinied, the Russian army was defecting, and the Italian army had collapsed. The war on the Western Front had developed into a stalemate, and Britain needed allies desperately. The future of Palestine and its population was a minor consideration compared to the immediate and desperate need for help. As a result of this desperation, Britain signed several conflicting agreements, which resulted in bitter disputes amongst Palestinian Arabs and the colonising Jews after WW1; this was still a problem when I arrived.

First there was the McMahon agreement, which promised the Arabs independence if they sided with Britain against the Germans and Ottomans, by opening up a new Eastern Front, and drawing vital resources and supplies away from the besieged western Front. I remember this, because it was Lawrence of Arabia and all of those goings on that we learnt about at school.

Then there was the Balfour declaration. German Zionists went to the British War Cabinet and offered to help encourage America to join the war and to stop funding the German war machine, on the guarantee that if America did join, then after the war the British would give them Palestine. This played to their talents, as they were bankers and media moguls, able to report anti German propaganda and change the mind-set of the civilian population.

These two promises were clearly incompatible. To complicate matters further, at the same time the British and French signed the secret Sykes Picot Agreement, which carved up the entire region after the war between themselves.

All these different and conflicting promises came to a head after WW1, when they were laid bare for everyone to see. The

Jews wanted to occupy 'their' land, but the Arabs disputed the fact that the land was theirs, and the Germans blamed the Jews for losing the war. To make things worse, in 1922, the League of Nations gave Britain administrative rule over Palestine, known as the British Mandate.

Before WW1, Jewish immigration to Palestine was slow, but was given a boost afterwards by the promise in the Balfour letter of a homeland. By the early 1930s, and the rise of National Socialism, life in Germany was becoming uncomfortable, with the Nazis boycotting Jewish shops and stores, removing them from positions of authority, and imprisoning them for political activism. As a result, Jews were leaving Germany for more welcoming lands. Many would have preferred to migrate to America, but it was virtually impossible unless they had wealth or a relative who was a citizen. The other alternative was to travel to other countries or Palestine; some did, but many stayed in Germany too long and were eventually unable to leave at all.

At first, thousands of Jews were permitted to immigrate to Palestine from all over the world. Predictably, Palestinian Arabs felt that their homeland was being threatened and Jews were occupying their land. Unable to redress their concerns, they rioted and attacked disputed Jewish land settlements. By 1936, the violence against Jews by Arab Palestinians had seriously escalated, and was ruthlessly repressed by British Troops.

By 1939, just prior to the outbreak of WW2, the British tried to address Arab concerns by reducing the number of immigrants allowed into Palestine to 15,000 annually. Once that quota was exceeded, Jews fleeing Nazi persecution were not allowed into Palestine, and instead were interned in detention camps or deported to places such as the island of Mauritius. To get around the ban, a clandestine immigration effort called *Aliya Bet* started, and involved tens of thousands of European Jews escaping the Nazis in boats and small ships. The Royal Navy intercepted many of the vessels, but an unknown number of them, which were unseaworthy, sank without trace or were wrecked.

The quota had not been well received by Jewish splinter groups. One group, which formed in 1940, was called the *Fighters for the Freedom of Israel*. We knew them as the *Stern Gang*, and they started what they described as a violent uprising against the British administration with the aim of driving them out of Palestine. They were not very active in violence at first, putting their efforts into robbing banks to raise funds and aid refugees. To begin with, the authorities described them as gangsters and thugs. That changed after they attempted, but failed, to assassinate the Head of the British Secret Police in Lod; they were then branded as terrorists.

I had arrived in a place that had spent years battling with the local Arabs and resisting migration against the will of the local Jewish population; it was no wonder no one liked or trusted the British after what we had started.

30
Sparrows

Palestine had not been affected too badly by the war. The Italians made a number of bombing raids in 1942 against Tel Aviv, and the oil installation at Haifa. Since then, it had been very peaceful, and the only real enemy was boredom. We spent most of our time playing cards and discussing the war in Europe; what was happening, how far inland we had pushed, how soon the war would end, and when we would be home.

I remember being alarmed to hear about a new weapon that had been launched against London. It was called the *Vergeltungswaffe 1*, the 'Vengeance Weapon Number One', or V-1 flying bomb. It became known as the buzz bomb, or 'doodlebug', because of the noise its engine made. It was an early cruise missile, and the first production aircraft to use a pulsejet for power. Thousands of these terror weapons were fired at London from launch facilities along the French Pas-de-Calais and Dutch coasts. We were all wondering when they would be aimed at us.

June was also the end of the rainy season, and the now-familiar fire prevention routine began. There was the constant risk of fire from discarded cigarette ends and broken glass. Because of this, all of the camp's grass and undergrowth had to be cut down and cleared away up to a distance of fifty feet from all wooden buildings and the petrol and ammunition stores. There was also the obligatory unit reorganisation. These were now happening so frequently that they took place without anyone really noticing. I was able to keep on top of what was going on and avoid getting too bored because I was riding dispatches between Regimental Headquarters and the Anti-Aircraft Defence Headquarters in Haifa and got to hear all the gossip.

An anti-theft trick that we had learnt in Cairo was to tie string around our AB 64 pay book and then attach the string to the bottom hole of our shirt pocket. This became adopted as an official form of dress, and we were all issued with white lanyards and instructions on how to wear them.

Then there was the annual round of 'take care' orders. We were reminded that having a camera was a privilege, and that we were forbidden from taking photographs of military equipment or installations. There was the threat of severe disciplinary action if we contravened that order.

We were prevented from bathing in any river within six miles of the coast, or any part of the Qindon River because of a new water hazard called 'Bilharzia'. This was transmitted by a type of water snail found in streams, lakes and ponds in Palestine. Added to this, the brothels along Farrow Street, and the passage leading into Heshon Street in Lower Haifa were designated out of bounds because of the risk of VD.

Dispatch riding still had its perks; not only did it get me away from the camp, but I also got to visit lots of sites in the region. My two favourite places to stop and laze away the day whenever I could were a cafe we called *Piccas*, and the *Piccadilly Mount Carmel* on Herzlio Street in Haifa; this was a popular meeting point for dispatch riders.

My secret getaway was the city of Tiberias on the west bank of the Sea of Galilee. It was about a one-hour ride from camp, and was always worth a detour and the risk of getting into trouble. Tiberias is the most relaxing and peaceful place I have ever been. At the time, that was mainly because in June and July it was too hot for people to visit or venture outside, as temperatures hovered in the nineties. It was one of the migration hotspots, with Jewish settlers moving into the area in large numbers, and the remaining Arab Palestinians moving out. But there was no trouble that I could see, and I would sit at my favourite lakeside cafe called *the British Cafe* for hours, sipping English tea and long cold drinks, served by Arab waiters in their white robes and red cummerbunds. The sparrows were so tame that they would sit on your shoulder and eat from your hand. There were also kingfishers everywhere, as common as starlings. Later in life I would always encourage birds into my garden, hoping to recreate those memories; I got lots of sparrows, but no kingfishers! Best of all was at dusk, when the temperature dropped and the white-sailed boats returned to the shore. Looking south, I would watch the last rays of light illuminate and then silhouette the mountains of Moab — a magnificent and very peaceful sight. Once the sun went down, I would jump on my bike and slowly ride back to camp, content and at peace with the world; this was not in a religious way, but rather resembled a feeling of being safe, and that no one was trying to kill me.

The habit of collecting 'Buckshee' stuff was still common practice, but it was not tolerated as much as it had been in the past. I still needed to scavenge spare parts for my bike which would be useful in the event of a breakdown, because they were always in short supply. Spare parts were also traded between riders at *Piccas*, often in exchange for booze, girlie-mags and rare, hard to get spare parts! Scrounging for military equipment was all part and parcel of my daily routine. Taking articles of personal equipment was taboo and always seen as stealing. It was a dishonest practice, and offenders would not only face harsh military discipline, but also rough justice from fists and boots from troops. Surprisingly, articles such as cups, saucers, glasses, plates, knives, forks and spoons from the NAAFI canteen were seen as fair game. But this was not the way the NAAFI saw it; they estimated that they lost over 100,000 pounds a year from theft.

In July, we started to store water in preparation for the expected shortages in the summer, and I was sent on refresher training on the new American Mark 3 Radar. In Burma, the sieges at Imphal and Kohima ended on the 20th July. Around about the same time, the remaining Anti-Aircraft sites on the North Africa coast were decommissioned, along with ten sites that were protecting Cairo.

On the 24th July, near the town of Lublin in Poland, the Soviet army came across the abandoned Majdanek concentration camp. The prisoners had been removed and marched to other camps ahead of the Russian advance. Majdanek was then burned in an attempt to mask its presence as the Germans retreated from the region. But the remains of gas chambers were evident, and this was the first major concentration camp discovered by those fighting against Germany. The evidence found was a brutal confirmation of the rumours of the existence of such camps. In the following weeks, Soviet troops went on to liberate the abandoned camps of Belzec, Sobibor and Treblinka.

I cannot remember exactly when I first started to hear reports about the Nazi atrocities and what became known as the Holocaust. At first, we listened in utter shock; the reports were hard to believe, and the Germans I had encountered on the battlefield seemed incapable of such things. I think that once they discovered more camps, it became widely and graphically reported in the newspapers and on news reels in the cinemas. Shortly after the discovery of Majdanek, Churchill said, "'I like the idea of the Jews trying to get the murderers of their fellow countrymen in Central Europe," and the British government consented to the establishment of a Palestinian Military Jewish Brigade. This would join the army in the fight against the Axis forces.

I was busy throughout the month of August. At the beginning, I helped escort the First Light Anti-Aircraft from Alexandria back to Haifa. I got to spend a few days in Alex, as the battery prepared for the move, and it was nice to be back on familiar ground.

On the 9th, the High Commissioner of Palestine, Sir Harold MacMichael, was travelling between Jerusalem and Jaffa when his car was ambushed by members of the Stern Gang. They sprayed his car with bullets and threw hand grenades, but he managed to escape with minor injuries. This was not the first assassination attempt on Sir Harold. He was blamed by the Jewish freedom fighters for the restrictions on immigration, and one incident in particular, back in 1942, when he refused to allow around 800 refugees aboard the SS Struma to enter into Palestine. When the ship sank in the Black Sea, he was held responsible for their deaths.

On the 21st, I was sent to the anti-aircraft school in Cairo to attend a Junior Non-Commissioned Officers course until the 3rd September. All I can remember is learning how to shout orders on the drill square and how to control a fire picket. I also learned that we were responsible for the health and hygiene of troops in our charge; this was mostly about recognising foot rot and how and where to build toilets.

With September, the autumn arrived, and brought about an environment of fear. On the 27th, there were coordinated attacks against police stations which were ransacked and weapons stolen, before being set on fire. A police superintendent was shot and killed in Tel-Aviv, and curfews were put in place across Palestine, with no movement in certain Jewish quarters after 4 p.m.

At the same time, the formation of the Jewish Brigade Group of the British Army that had been agreed in July, was established in Egypt. It included more than 5,000 Jewish volunteers and was made up of two infantry battalions and a Royal Artillery Field Regiment.

Around this time, Arab Heads of State met in Alexandria and issued a statement called the Alexandria Protocol, which set out the Arab position. They made it clear that, although they regretted the bitter fate inflicted upon European Jewry by European dictatorships, the issue of European Jewish survivors ought not to be confused with Zionism. Solving the problem of European Jewry, they asserted, should not be achieved by inflicting injustice on Palestinian Arabs.

On the 4th October, I contracted an infection in both eyes, probably caused by poorly disinfected water in a swimming pool in Haifa. I was in considerable pain, and because the medical officer was unable to treat me, I was given orders to report to the eye hospital in Cairo. I was unable to ride my bike or drive myself there, but, unsurprisingly, there was no-end of volunteers willing to take me to Cairo. Alas, no one could be released, and I had to make my own way, by whatever transport became available. In some ways, avoiding driving on the roads was a good idea. October was the start of the rainy season, and the roads became very dangerous. This was because, throughout the dry season, a great deal of dust and oil stuck to the road surface. Once the rain came, this mixture formed a very greasy type of mud which was extremely slippery and lethal to motorcycles and anyone trying to stop in a hurry.

31
The Desert Fox Dies

I don't remember much about the journey to Cairo; I know I was in considerable discomfort, that I got there by train, and that I was very glad when I arrived at the British Military Hospital (BMH) and started to receive treatment. I spent several days in a darkened room, and was given regular eye drops and ointments. Although the pain stopped very quickly, I was extremely sensitive to sunlight and they gave me some RAF anti-dazzle sunglasses with side shields to wear. I was then discharged from the main hospital and moved to a convalescent ward for rest and recovery. Over the next few weeks, I spent my days relaxing around Cairo and doing the best I could to prolong my stay. Unfortunately, all too soon I was given the all clear and orders to return to Palestine.

I remember exactly where I was when I heard that Erwin Rommel, the 'Desert Fox', had died. It was the 15th October, and I was with a few of the lads from the convalescent ward drinking afternoon tea at the Service Club, in the Ezbekieh Gardens.

We heard that a few months earlier in July, Rommel had been wounded when his car was attacked by a fighter plane in France. He had returned home to recover from his injuries, but had succumbed to his wounds and died on the 14th October. It may seem strange to say, but we were all a little saddened by the news. He was a respected German officer; we even talked about him as a *super military leader* — before we beat him at El

Alamein that is! To many 'Desert Rats', Rommel epitomised a gentleman's approach to the deadly issue of war.

Most of the stories going around involved the way he treated POWs. One I remember being told was about some Italian troops who had taken watches and other valuables from their British captives. When Rommel found out, he ordered that they be returned to their owners immediately.

We only learnt the truth about his death after the war. He had been wounded in an attack and returned home, but he was also implicated in the failed July 1944 Bomb Plot to kill Hitler. Rommel actually committed suicide after Hitler promised that his family would not be punished for his indiscretions if he were to die *of his wounds*. The fact that he had been part of a plot to kill Hitler only furthered my belief that he was one of the good Germans.

In mid-October, I returned to Palestine, taking the long route back, which included a leisurely cruise on a barge up the Nile before catching a train from Port Said to Haifa.

I had only been gone for a few weeks, but a lot had happened in that time. The main topic of conversation was that all the brothels in Haifa had been designated out of bounds because they were infested with lice and VD was prevalent. Those who had been caught 'indulging' had received fourteen days' pay deduction from their wages. A few had been caught a second time, and had received the same fine plus three days in the jail, which was un-affectionately known as the 'glass house'.

What affected me most was not the loss of brothels, but access to some of the remote areas that I visited whilst delivering dispatches. They were seen as being unsafe following the continued and escalating attacks against the British establishment and had also been designated out of bounds. This included the English Cafe in Tierias, which made me very sad; although I did continue to drop-in on a couple of occasions, eventually I stopped going altogether.

The attacks came from both Jewish and Arab gangs, and the locals called them bandits or terrorists, depending on which side they were on. At this stage, we still referred to them as gangsters, and despite both sides being involved, most of the trouble was blamed on a few Jewish gangs. What didn't help were reports that one gang had carried out an attack wearing British army uniforms.

Despite this, there was a lot of respect for the Jewish plight, but the hooliganish behaviour of a few started to impact on the way military personnel treated the Jewish community as a whole.

On the 26th October, the security level went up, and as well as my service revolver, I was re-issued my trusted Thompson machine-gun. I had to provide details of my route and timings to RHQ whenever carrying Top Secret dispatches anywhere in Palestine and the Transjordan area to the east of the Jordan River.

The shootings and bombings continued in Haifa and Tel-Aviv; there was even an attempt to capture the civilian radio station at Ramallah. On the 6th November, Lord Moyne, the British

Minister of State for the Middle East, was assassinated by a Jewish gang and all *resistance* then became classed as terrorism. The three main Jewish gangs, Haganah, IZL and the Stern Gang, all united to form the *Jewish Resistance Movement*, and the terrorist attacks and bombings against the British administration escalated. It was almost as if the war had stopped and our new world was about shootings, arrests, arms running and political warfare amongst the Jews and Arabs. Palestine was an open wound, and we did our best to keep out of the way.

Some dispatch riders were reporting that they were being targeted by snipers. It never happened to me, or if they had been shooting at me, I never heard the shots. Everything changed, however, when a dispatch rider was decapitated by a fine steel wire stretched neck-high between two trees. The wire-across-the-road trap eventually led to vehicles being fitted with a sword like steel blade attached to the front end, but not on motorbikes. Dispatch riding stopped being as much fun from then on. To make things worse, the NAAFI would refuse to sell anything other than a cuppa char to anyone who was not stationed in their camp, which meant I often went hungry.

On the 1st December, the regiment was on the move again, this time a few miles south of Haifa to No.2 Practice Camp just below Mount Carmel. Although the RHQ tried to remain in the city at the Saltzman Hotel, they were eventually sent packing on the 8th, and we joined the main unit at the practice camp.

The brigade held a raffle; it was a very exciting event, as the winners would be flown back to England for Christmas. Two lads from the regiment were drawn, Gunners 'Spud' Mitchell and 'Ted' Newcome.

December started with the lifting of the nightly blackout, just in time for the Jewish festival of Hanukkah, the Feast of the Lights. The seven-branched candelabras were lit, not only in Jewish homes, but on the rooftops of synagogues, public buildings and the water towers. At the same time, police carried out what they called an anti-terrorist operation in the seaside resort of Bat Yam, south of Jaffa. Several hundred men were detained and taken to interrogation centres. Although we were not involved with the arrests on the 5th December, I was involved with moving fourteen gangsters from the interrogation centre in Haifa to the airport, where they were flown to Cairo to be tried.

Back at camp, we became known as the Second HAA Canine Fraternisation Battery. Wherever there are troops, there will almost certainly be dogs, and the camp was no exception. It was full of dogs that had had a succession of different owners as troops came and went. Most were friendly, but there were also some wild dogs, which we called *Pi-Dogs*. They roamed the camp, hunting and scavenging in packs and were very dangerous; there was also the ever-present danger of rabies and occasionally anthrax.

As part of the festive celebrations, we held the traditional inter-regimental football and boxing matches. The commanding officer decided, for a change, to have a gymkhana as well, the highlight of which would be a dog race.

The idea was simple enough; the dogs were held at one end of the football pitch and their owners stood at the other end waving the dog's favourite treat and shouting encouragement. Everyone else placed bets on who would win and, to the sound of brouhaha, the dogs were released. But, instead of the dogs going to their owners, they were intercepted by *Pi-Dogs* and they started to attack each other. It was absolute mayhem in the middle of the field and it took ages to halt the fracas. Once they had been separated, the sight was quite harrowing, with some of the dogs dead or dying; to make things worse, the CO ordered that all dogs on the camp were to be destroyed.

Our HQ moved from the camp and set itself up in a little village called Amyun — a beautiful location about ten miles away from the Lebanon Mountains. Normally they were snow-covered all year round for about three quarters of a mile down from the summit, but the December of 1944 was exceptionally cold and the village became trapped in snow, meaning we had to transport supplies using mules. I was able to smuggle one dog, a popular small black and white terrier, out of the camp before the cull started, and I left it with the HQ signal section for safe keeping. I stayed with them for a few days before heading back to camp. It was very cold, and they got firewood by chopping down part of the olive grove and some telegraph poles. One of the officers had a guitar, and at night we all sat round a camp fire and sang songs.

On the 17th December, a note appeared on the regimental notice board. They were looking for volunteers to train as glider pilots. The idea did appeal to me, but applicants who had completed more than two and a half years of overseas service were barred from applying.

There was an organised pilgrimage to Bethlehem to visit the Holy sites over Christmas, and there were plenty of films and entertainment laid on. I remember that the *Great Dictator* was a popular film; it was constantly doing the rounds, and I must have seen it a dozen times or more. There were also two American cartoons; one was about a silly soldier called Private Snafu. *Snafu* was an abbreviation of Situation Normal, All Fouled Up, and the cartoon warned about the dangers of booby-traps. The other was a Walt Disney propaganda film called *Education In Death* — *a story about how German children became Nazis.*

We also started a new training programme alongside some African infantry soldiers, which consisted of military, fitness and internal security training. Added to this, there was optional education in subjects such as leather work, book keeping, automobile engineering, boot repairing and languages such as French. Because I was still on dispatch duties, I was exempt from the education subjects.

Christmas soon came and went, and the New Year brought new rules and new adventures.

32
Marching Home

In the January of 1945, the regiment was placed on seven days' standby to be deployed anywhere in the Middle East theatre, and we practiced antiaircraft gunnery drills daily. We also underwent training as infantry soldiers so we could be called upon to assist with 'internal security' operations if needed. There was also some kind of physical fitness activity, including route marches in full battle kit, every morning.

Good order and military discipline descended on the camp to everyone's horror. Despite still being at war in a far-off distant country, you would have thought we were back in England and at a training depot. We hadn't saluted officers for years; this was because they didn't want to be signalled out to a sniper. The situation changed completely, and we were saluting anything that moved, even snapping to attention and saluting them as they entered or left the camp. It seemed a great idea to me; let the snipers shoot the officer first! So, I would salute and give them a great big smile as well — I don't think they ever realised why I appeared so happy.

The Royal Engineers arrived and using diggers cleared some ground and made a parade square. The Regimental Sergeant Major (RSM) and the sergeants took great pleasure in marching us up and down the parade square shouting and screaming at the tops of their voices. Sometimes they would try and make us laugh so that they could shout at us even more for smiling on parade. They all carried canes or swagger sticks which they used to poke us with. They would come out with silly sayings like, "I'm going to shove this stick through your ears and ride you round this parade square like a shagging motorbike," or "I will stick-it up your bum hole and turn you into a lollypop." They would also poke you in the chest and say, "There is a piece of shit on the end of my stick and it's not this end." Another favourite was when you didn't swing your arms correctly when marching or when saluting. They would scream, "I'm going to rip your arm off and slap you around the head with the soggy end." The main qualification for being a drill sergeant was the ability to shout and swear without stopping for at least thirty minutes. They even found a bugler and we had to learn the different bugle calls by humming and whistling them to each other until we knew them off by heart. The ones I can still remember are the fire alarm, stand-to at the double, reveillie, and the mail call.

Towards the end of January, we heard that the Russians had come across another German concentration camp, but this time it was still occupied. The stories of what happened there and pictures in the press were horrific; the camp was called Auschwitz.

We were starting to get reports about bandits who, on horse back, would sneak into villages at night, kidnap people and demand a ransom for their release. Once the ransom was paid, they allegedly cut the throats of their victims so they could not identify the villains. As if the worry of getting my head sliced off by a wire trap or shot at by a sniper was not bad enough, I was now fearful of being kidnapped by bandits whilst delivering dispatches.

One day in mid-February we were sitting around outside one of the tents playing cards, when someone suddenly shouted out "Bloody 'ell Bandits!" I instinctively grabbed my rifle along with the other 'old timers', whilst the brown knees just froze to the ground. There were about twelve of us and around sixty armed Arabs on horse back, in a long column trotting straight towards us. As they got nearer, I could see they had Lee Enfield rifles slung over their shoulders and leather ammunition bandoliers across their chests. Some also had long swords strapped on the side of their saddles. It was like watching a silent movie as they moved towards us. I had no intention of getting my throat cut, and was ready to go out all guns blazing. I could hear the thud of hooves on the sand getting louder and louder as the mounted group drew ever closer, when one of the lads cocked his gun ready to fire; at this point, the sergeant shouted out, "Hold your fire." We watched them and they watched us as they sailed past us and disappeared as quickly as they had arrived. We found out later that they were not bandits but cavalry of The Arab Legion's Transjordan Frontier Force, commanded by General Glubb Pasha; they were tasked throughout Palestine, predominantly with guarding military depots and airfields. It was a good job the sergeant knew who they were, otherwise we would have ended up shooting at each other.

Turkey had remained a neutral country during WW2; this changed in February, when they entered the war on the side of the allies against Germany and Japan. We immediately started to load all our guns and stores onto trains with the expectation that we would soon be moving into Turkey. At the same time, we started to hear rumours that we were going to join forces in France.

On the 21st March, the trains pulled out of Haifa railway yard, and instead of heading east towards Turkey, we headed west. Our orders were to make our way to Alexandria, Egypt, where we would board troop ships and sail back to England.

33
Blighty

We spent the next three weeks in a transit camp just outside Alexandria, waiting for our orders to disembark. There were lots of rumours that we were not going home and that we would instead be heading east to join the fight against the Japanese. When we did eventually board a troop ship for the two-week voyage back to Blighty, despite all the reassurances that we were going home, I remember being worried that the boat would change course, and that I would wake one morning to find us sailing down the Suez Canal en route to Bombay instead of Glasgow.

We set sail on 22nd April 1945, the same day that the Russian army entered the outskirts of Berlin, and we knew then that the war would soon be over. Whilst at sea on the 28th, we heard that the Italian Prime Minister, Benito Mussolini, had been captured by partisans whilst trying to escape to Switzerland. Mussolini, his mistress Clara Piazzale and twelve others were summarily executed and their bodies taken back to Milan where they were hung upside down on public display in the Piazzale Loreto.

A few days later, on the 30th, we heard that Adolf Hitler had committed suicide and that Admiral Karl Dönitz had become the President of Germany.

We had a special church service on the deck of the ship on Sunday 6th to mark the end of hostilities. However, it took another week before Germany surrendered unconditionally at the Allied Headquarters in Rheims on the 7th May, the same day our ship arrived into Glasgow.

We had expected to be released on leave as soon as we landed, but instead we were ordered to make our way by train to our new barracks in Leigh-on-Sea in Essex, before being released.

Just after breakfast, the whole regiment made its way reluctantly to the train station; to add to the misery, we were given a palliasse pillow and told to fill it with straw. We soon learned that this was to be our only comfort during a two-day train journey. The train had only a few windows, wooden seats, and of course no toilets. So, we stopped every few hours for food and toileting.

At one minute after midnight on the 8th May, 1945, a ceasefire took effect and the war in Europe was over — a day generally known as Victory in Europe Day, or VE Day. Whilst the country was celebrating the end of the war, I was stuck on a train, tormented by the sound of celebrations and church bells ringing as we passed through towns and cities. It was all too much for three of the lads, who jumped off the train and went AWOL. They had been away from home for years, and rather than wait to get to our destination and be released on leave, as the train passed through their home towns they said their goodbyes and slipped away.

We arrived in Leigh-on-Sea in the late afternoon to be met by a thunderstorm; we stood around freezing for ages whilst trucks transported us along the sea front to Shoeburyness Artillery Barracks. We quickly dumped our kit, collected our pay, and went into town to join in the celebrations. I remember we put money into our sergeant's hat and piled into a pub; he shouted out "Thirty beers please, keeper," and that continued at each pub we arrived at throughout the evening. Apart from drinking a lot, I remember there was a bonfire, and that they made a fuss about turning the streetlights back on, as the town band played the Vera Lyn classics, 'There'll Always Be An England' and 'Land Of Hope And Glory'. We sang along, the loudest of all, to our different versions of Lili Marlene.

The next day, with a heavy hangover, I was issued with a train warrant and transported back to the railway station with orders to return to barracks on the 18th. VE Day had been turned into a public holiday; with that, and with train drivers not making it into work, it took nearly the whole day to get home. The celebrations soon ended, and for those at home it was back to the reality of day-to-day living and surviving on what rations they were given. Friends and family were more interested in tending vegetables on their allotments rather than spending the day in the pub, listening to my war stories. There were so many people who had lost friends and family, and it was hard talking to those whose loved ones were never coming back. I had spent years looking forward to getting back home, but it never lived up to the dream. As much as I hated the army, I missed my mates and was actually glad when it was time to head back to camp.

I returned on time, and we spent a few nervous weeks wondering what would happen next. There was still fighting in the Far East and the Pacific, and there was the real possibility of redeployment. We jokingly redefined the acronym for the British Liberation Army (BLA), which was the military designation for the force sent into action; this was changed to 'Burma Looms Ahead'. We were all relieved in June, when the regiment became part of the Fortieth Anti-Aircraft Brigade with orders to stay in England and to take-over the gun positions from the 126th Heavy Anti-Aircraft Regiment, which was being disbanded. On the 17th, they handed over all their guns, vehicles and stores, and we occupied their field locations at various sites in the Tendring, Weeley area, as well as sites to the east of Dovercourt by the sea.

I was attached to RHQ and given dispatch rider duties; life was great, and I adjusted to life back in England quickly. We were free to 'walk out' when off duty — a luxury that had been denied for so long; married men were also allowed to 'sleep out'. It would be a while before we would be awarded our campaign medals for service, but we were given medal ribbons to wear on our uniforms. I was a proud 'Desert Rat' with a ribbon to prove it. This also meant that, to stand out in the crowd, I and my mates would wear our hats at a ridiculous angle; I would pull the cap badge over my ear and wear suede desert boots. They soon banned us from 'showing off' and we had to wear issue shoes and our hats fitted properly, with the cap badge over the left eye — at least until we were out of sight of the camp that is!

Another habit which was hard to change was stealing cookhouse crockery; I don't know why, as we didn't need to, but some habits were just too hard to stop. The government reintroduced petrol rationing for civilians, and the theft of petrol for personal use or to sell on the black market increased significantly. Also, the roads suddenly became very busy with inexperienced drivers, and dispatch riding quickly became more hazardous.

In early July, 'Digger' Densham, who was one of the three who jumped the train back in May, was caught and returned to camp. He had been 'on the run' for about two months. They punished him with fourteen days' detention and a posting to Germany to join what would become the British Army On the Rhine (BAOR). He was sent with others to help with internal security, the disposal of war material, and the repatriation of prisoners of war and displaced persons. He was not alone; a few of the lads volunteered to go and left with kit bags full of banned foodstuff, cigarettes, and other contraband to trade and a hope that they would make their fortune somehow.

July also marked the start of the demobilisation early release scheme, and I applied for release to become a labourer on my sister's farm. Farming was listed as being a 'key occupational skill', so I was hopeful. However, I was rejected, as two German prisoners of war had been allocated to work on the farm, so I was not needed. It was unfortunate, and as even more German and Italian prisoners of war were brought over and allocated to agriculture and construction work, mine and others' chances of getting demobbed early were dashed.

There was also a general election held on 5th July, although the results were not declared until the 26th because of the time it took to transport the votes of those serving overseas. The result was an unexpected landslide victory for Clement Attlee's Labour Party, over Winston Churchill's Conservatives. It was the first time the Conservatives had lost the popular vote since the 1906 election — they would not win it again until 1955.

August saw the start of demobilisation, and around a dozen lads left; I wished them well and we promised that we would meet up once I got out. That never happened; despite all that we had been through together, life just got in the way of reunions.

On the 6th August, the United States dropped a nuclear bomb on the Japanese city of Hiroshima, followed by another on the 9th on Nagasaki. After that, on the 15th, the Japanese surrendered on what we remember as VJ Day, although the formal surrender ceremony was performed in Tokyo Bay, Japan, aboard the battleship USS Missouri on the 2nd September. The world war was now over, which we thought would speed-up the release process.

My world was shattered when, on the 18th August, my closest mate, John Wade, was killed whilst delivering dispatches. We had both become DRs at the same time, and his loss hit me hard. He was due to be released the following month, and had been making plans to get married. On the 24th, I was a member of the guard of honour, and he was laid to rest in Colchester cemetery.

There were lots of road traffic accidents, thankfully not all fatal ones. The main reason was that road surfaces were different throughout Britain. Each county was responsible for building and maintaining their own roads, influenced by local needs. In some areas, the roads were still dominated by pedestrians, bicycles, trams and omnibuses. Motorised vehicles were relatively new to the roads, and with the exception of a network of trunk roads that had been constructed after the First World War, many roads had a variety of different tar and bituminous surfaces. Once you left the trunk roads you could be faced with a variety of differently constructed 'Macadam' broken stone and tar surfaces, or even cobbled and, in some places, wooden-block paving. Whilst they were all challenging to drive on, once they got wet or were exposed to hot summer days, they became lethal, especially when stopping at speed.

The August Bank Holiday was cancelled. The reason given was that, "Civilians needed to travel in comfort and that too many troops heading home would cause bottlenecks at the transport hubs and overcrowd the buses and trains. Besides, we could take leave anytime." I remember being very angry about not being able to travel, as we had planned to spend the holidays in London.

By September the discharge of troops had become part of our normal routine, and men leaving had little impact day-to-day, but the churn of officers was more noticeable. Whenever a new one arrived, they would demand new ways of doing things and the constant change was making everyone grumpy. The many problems included theft of kit; nothing was safe. When people left they had to hand in issued stuff. Anything that was missing was deducted from your pay, so people would just 'grab and go'.

On the 12th September we received warning orders to move to the Liverpool area. This made me very happy because of the promise of a better social life, and a better rail network, which was welcome as everyone was constantly getting back late from leave because of the trains and being fined for a late return. Not everyone was happy with the move. One of the clerks in RHQ who handled the dispatches, 'CJ' Denshen, had a sweetheart in town; the thought of leaving her was too much, and so he went AWOL, but they caught him hiding in a coal shed a week later. He received 28 days in jail for his trouble, and still had to go to Liverpool.

In October we completely dismantled the camp. Previously we had handed everything over to an incoming unit; this was completely different, and much harder. Everything was either taken with us or handed back to its owners; pianos and snooker tables were returned to the NAAFI, and other leisure equipment, such as books, records and the like were sent to the YMCA and WVS.

For the move, I was on convoy duties, and between the 3rd and 5th I helped guide the regiment via Lutterworth to various sites around Liverpool. Things didn't start off well; 'Tweety' Bird had a motorcycle accident just outside Huntingdon shortly after we set off and ended up in hospital. On the second day, we passed within a few miles of home, and I was able to take a detour for an hour, but nearly got caught.

I was stationed with RHQ and the Twenty-eighth Battery in Moore Camp, Warrington, known as 'H20'. Twentieth Battery was at Heron Road Camp 'H29' in Meols, on the Birkenhead peninsular, and Sixteenth Battery was at 'H25', which was Chester. Shortly after we arrived, the Twenty-eighth Battery moved to Hutton Camp, Thurstaston on the Wirral.

We then fell into a familiar routine; we had the usual warnings about VD being a problem in Manchester, and lectures on the Official Secrets Act, with specific references to radar; I also got into a fight in the Milk Bar Cafe in Warrington. I escaped the Military Police, but Harry Porter and Eddie Squibb were charged with causing a disturbance and Johnny Hall for using insubordinate language and showing a threatening attitude to the police. They were fined three days' pay and spent most of November in a working party at the Sixty-ninth Ordinance Depot at Arrowe Park. I would go and see them whenever I visited Twentieth Battery, delivering their mail and the latest news.

Christmas came and went; we all received another two medal ribbons — the 1939 - 45 Star and Defence medal. I had still not received my demobilisation orders.

At the end of February I was posted to Sixteenth Battery, and three months later to Twenty-eighth Battery who were now based at Irby on the Wirral; then, on the 14th June, I was posted back to RHQ, and received my release notification.

A significant event which happened some time during May, 1946, and which I remember well, was when I had an accident whilst delivering dispatches between Chester and Irby. I was travelling along the main trunk road just outside Chester and was overtaking a car when, without any warning or indication, it turned right as I was passing. I had to swerve to avoid hitting the car and ended up in a ditch on the other side of the road. I was okay, but the bike was damaged. The driver was a community nurse doing her morning rounds; she had been distracted, and when she suddenly realised she was

about to miss her turning, she swerved across the road having not seen me overtaking. The regiment held a court of inquiry and I was not hopeful of a positive outcome, as the army deemed that the driver was always culpable in any road traffic accident, which meant you were already guilty before the trial started. However, the nurse presented herself at the court and explained how the accident had been completely her fault and I could have done nothing to stop it happening. To her credit, she didn't have to give evidence, but she came on her own accord and her attendance meant I was found not guilty.
.

On the 14th July, I had my release medical and was found to be fit and well; following this, on the 3rd August 1946, I was fitted out with a new 'demob' suit, shoes, a hat, and a train ticket home. I took a kit bag with all my military clobber in because I was on the reserve list and told to maintain it in good order for further duties if necessary. I did not officially finish until November because I had accumulated fifty-six days' release leave and forty days' overseas leave; on the 8th November 1946, my war service finally came to an end after five years and eleven months.

On my release papers, they provided a testimonial or reference to my service. They said my conduct had been good and summed up my service in just twenty words: *A cheerful and industrious type. Has a mechanical turn of mind. Has done well as a dispatch rider. Quite reliable.*

Afterword

Fred returned home, in the words of Kipling, as a "time-expired soldier with service to 'is name." Like many others who had served their time on the front line, he was a casualty of war — these were men whose minds had been brutalised by the sights and smells of death, the terror of modern warfare, and the killing.

Thousands of men like Fred, who had served in front line units, were dealing with the same battle-induced trauma which today is recognised as an illness, Post Traumatic Stress Disorder (PTSD). But when Fred was demobilised, people didn't talk about what was going on in their minds. It was just not the done-thing; you simply straightened your shoulders and got on with life, having to deal with any issues yourself.

Today, thankfully, veterans who bear the psychological scars of combat are treated with greater understanding and respect. But that was not the case for Fred; as well as having to cope with the terrible things he had witnessed, he also suffered from feelings of guilt because so many of his comrades had not made it home, but he had. The images of suffering went on to haunt him for many years, and he often struggled with his bottled-up emotions; sometimes, these emotions would result in angry outbursts, or him just cutting himself off from everyone. He also returned home having forgotten the rules of ordinary society — a society not governed by his constant awareness of the need to survive. He opposed authority whenever and wherever it raised its head, choosing to remain close only to a few friends — those he found to be dependable.

One of the ways he coped was by turning his back on the war; this meant cutting all contact with those that he had served.

On leaving the service, he first worked as a labourer on Goodrest Farm, Hunnington, just outside Birmingham, which was his sister's farm. He met a local girl, Gwendoline 'Gwen' Booton, who lived half a mile away in Red Hill Place. Romance blossomed, and they married on the 16th April 1947. Just before Christmas the following year, on the 17th December 1948, Gwen gave birth to a girl, Maureen Susanne. With a baby on the way, Fred wanted to earn extra money and sought other employment. He briefly worked as a gardener at the Old School House, Neen Savage in Cleobury Mortimer, before finally getting a job at the Halesowen Foundry as a machine moulder, where he worked until his retirement. Gwen was with him when he left the services and he needed support and comfort most, but she betrayed him for another man; she left the family home and Maureen, and divorce quickly followed.

Fred eventually found happiness with Margaret, and they married on the 27th July 1957. Margaret already had a son, Keith, who was four years old at the time, and with Maureen aged eight, they put two bad past relationships together to make a great one.

Margaret, without being aware of what she was achieving, was the one who nursed him back to normality. He never fully ditched the last remnants of his nightmares; he continued to reject authority, and was sometimes accused of having a lack of compassion and of seeing the world from nobody's side but his own. It was only after many years that he realised that his condition was treated with great compassion and care by those he loved, and how much heartache and misery his anger had caused to those he loved.

Fred's war had been dominated by his service in North Africa and Palestine, and he had been saddened by its decline in the 1950s. Despite the fact that the war had left Egypt richer than it had been before, the end of the hostilities saw considerable change in Egypt. Industry, which had thrived when supporting the war effort, was in decline; wages remained low, and food prices increased.

Despite Britain and others owing Egypt millions of pounds for supplies, damages and compensation, all the wealth was going to the rich and not to the poor which provided fertile ground for every extremist and nationalist group.

In September 1947, the United Nations partitioned Palestine and the British mandate ended in May 1948. Immediately, the Arab states, represented by Egypt, Iraq, Transjordan and Syria, invaded Palestine in an attempt to halt the state of Israel, and in Cairo Jewish businesses were attacked. Finally, any hopes of Fred returning to Cairo to revisit familiar surroundings were dashed on the 26th January 1952 — Black Saturday. On that day, gangs started attacking and burning buildings which had any connection to foreign investors; cinemas, bars and shops were destroyed, and many people were killed. Shepheard's hotel and Madam Badia's Opera Casino and Restaurant were amongst the first to be set on fire; the Turf Club, Barclay's Bank and the Morris Motors car show room were also destroyed, as well as many other British-owned offices.

However, this story started out as a quest to re-unite Fred with his medals, and that was achieved. He got the chance to wear them with pride on Remembrance Sunday, 2013.

NON-FICTION FROM APS PUBLICATIONS

Bella In The Wych-Elm (Andrew Sparke)
Croc Curry & Texas Tea: Surviving Nigeria (Paul Dickinson)
Istanbul: The Visitor Essentials (Andrew Sparke)
Piggery Jokery In Tonga (Andrew Sparke)
Rear Gunner(Andrew Sparke)
Stutthof (Andrew Sparke)
The Strange Free-Fall Of Fred Ryland (Helen Pitt)
The Ways Of Mevagissey (Andrew Sparke)
War Shadows (Andrew Sparke)

PHOTOGRAPHICS
Images (Andrew Sparke)
Istanbul In Pictures (Andrew Sparke)
Shapely Curves and Bumpers (Lee Benson)
Wild Life (David Kiteley)

www.andrewsparke.com

26323816R00149

Printed in Great Britain
by Amazon